Herbs &
Spices

Jean Paré

companyscoming.com
visit our ↖ website

Front Cover

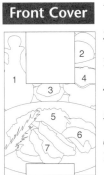

1. Tarragon Garlic Vinegar, page 132
2. Fresh Herb Cheese Rolls, page 46
3. Garlic And Chive Butter, page 124
4. Vanilla Bean Fruit Salad, page 139
5. Pistachio And Apricot Pilaf, page 111
6. Herb Sauce, page 121
7. Garlic Rosemary Lamb, page 96

Back Cover

1. Feta Herb Bread, page 43
2. Fresh Herb Tea, page 41
3. Spicy Yam Soup, page 64

Props Courtesy Of:
Casa Bugatti
Island Pottery Inc.

Props Courtesy Of:
Cherison Enterprises Inc.
The Bay

We gratefully acknowledge the following suppliers for their generous support of our Test Kitchen and Photo Studio:

Broil King Barbecues   Lagostina ®
Corelle ®   Proctor Silex ® Canada
Hamilton Beach ® Canada   Tupperware ®

Herbs & Spices

Third Printing September 2004

National Library of Canada Cataloguing in Publication
Paré, Jean
    Herbs & spices : savour the flavour / Jean Paré.

(Orginal series)
Includes index.
ISBN 1-896891-84-5

    1. Cookery (Herbs) 2. Cookery (Spices). I. Title. II. Title: Herbs and spices. III. Series: Paré, Jean. Original series.

TX819.H4P37 2004   641.6'57   C2004-901696-2

Published by
Company's Coming Publishing Limited
2311 – 96 Street
Edmonton, Alberta, Canada T6N 1G3
Tel: 780-450-6223 Fax: 780-450-1857
www.companyscoming.com

Company's Coming is a registered trademark owned by Company's Coming Publishing Limited

Printed in Canada

Visit us on-line

companyscoming.com

| Who We Are | Browse Cookbooks | Cooking Tonight? | Home |

everyday ingredients

feature recipes

feature recipes — Cooking tonight? Check out this month's **feature recipes**— absolutely FREE!

tips and tricks — Looking for some great kitchen helpers? **tips and tricks** are here to save the day!

reader circle — In search of answers to cooking or household questions? Do you have answers you'd like to share? Join the fun with **reader circle**, our on-line question and answer bulletin board. Great for swapping recipes too!

cooking links — Other interesting and informative web-sites are just a click away with **cooking links.**

cookbook search — Find cookbooks by title, description or food category using **cookbook search**.

contact us — We want to hear from you—**contact us** lets you offer suggestions for upcoming titles, or share your favourite recipes.

Company's Coming
COOKBOOKS®

Canada's
most popular cookbooks!

Company's Coming Cookbook Series

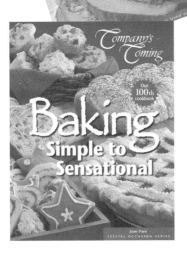

Original Series

- Softcover, 160 pages
- 6" x 9" (15 cm x 23 cm) format
- Lay-flat binding
- Full colour photos
- Nutrition information

Quick & easy recipes, everyday ingredients!

Lifestyle Series

- Softcover, 160 pages
- 8" x 10" (20 cm x 25 cm) format
- Paperback & spiral binding
- Full colour photos
- Nutrition information

Most Loved Recipe Collection

- Hardcover, 128 pages
- 8 3/4" x 8 3/4" (22 cm x 22 cm) format
- Full colour throughout
- Nutrition information

Special Occasion Series

- Hardcover & softcover, 192 pages
- 8 1/2" x 11" (22 cm x 28 cm) format
- Durable sewn binding
- Full colour throughout
- Nutrition information

See page 157 for a complete listing of cookbooks or visit companyscoming.com

Table of Contents

The Company's Coming Story

Jean Paré grew up understanding that the combination of family, friends and home cooking is the essence of a good life. From her mother she learned to appreciate good cooking, while her father praised even her earliest attempts. When she left home she took with her many acquired family recipes, a love of cooking and an intriguing desire to read recipe books like novels!

"never share a recipe you wouldn't use yourself"

In 1963, when her four children had all reached school age, Jean volunteered to cater the 50th anniversary of the Vermilion School of Agriculture, now Lakeland College. Working out of her home, Jean prepared a dinner for over 1000 people which launched a flourishing catering operation that continued for over eighteen years. During that time she was provided with countless opportunities to test new ideas with immediate feedback—resulting in empty plates and contented customers! Whether preparing cocktail sandwiches for a house party or serving a hot meal for 1500 people, Jean Paré earned a reputation for good food, courteous service and reasonable prices.

"Why don't you write a cookbook?" Time and again, as requests for her recipes mounted, Jean was asked that question. Jean's response was to team up with her son, Grant Lovig, in the fall of 1980 to form Company's Coming Publishing Limited. April 14, 1981 marked the debut of "150 DELICIOUS SQUARES," the first Company's Coming cookbook in what soon would become Canada's most popular cookbook series.

Jean Paré's operation has grown steadily from the early days of working out of a spare bedroom in her home. Full-time staff includes marketing personnel located in major cities across Canada. Home Office is based in Edmonton, Alberta in a modern building constructed specially for the company.

Today the company distributes throughout Canada and the United States in addition to numerous overseas markets, all under the guidance of Jean's daughter, Gail Lovig. Best-sellers many times over in English, Company's Coming cookbooks have also been published in French and Spanish. Familiar and trusted in home kitchens around the world, Company's Coming cookbooks are offered in a variety of formats, including the original softcover series.

Jean Paré's approach to cooking has always called for quick and easy recipes using everyday ingredients. Even when travelling, she is constantly on the lookout for new ideas to share with her readers. At home, she can usually be found researching and writing recipes, or working in the company's test kitchen. Jean continues to gain new supporters by adhering to what she calls "the golden rule of cooking:" never share a recipe you wouldn't use yourself. It's an approach that works—*millions of times over!*

Foreword

Have you ever brought home a new herb or spice only to realize you didn't know what food it would complement? Well, dust off those jars because *Herbs & Spices* will release the unfamiliar flavours relegated to the back of your cupboard into new dishes that will fast become family favourites!

Herbs refresh and cleanse the palate and spices tantalize the tongue. Enjoy both in *Herbs & Spices*, a collection of quick and easy recipes that will introduce you to exotic aromas or help rejuvenate favourite standbys.

Is there anything more delectable than a seasoned stew or a spicy chili simmering on the stove? Not unless it's the aroma from an herbed bread baking in the oven. Enhance foods by adding herbs and spices, but use sparingly so their flavour doesn't overpower the food's natural taste. The amount of an herb or spice can be increased, decreased, left out or substituted according to personal preference. Cilantro, for example, is one of those herbs that people either love or hate, so change the amount to your liking, or substitute the same amount of parsley. I invite you to season to taste in our recipes.

In many of these recipes, you can substitute fresh herbs for dried. The general rule of thumb is to use 1/4 tsp. (1 mL) dried for every 1 tsp. (5 mL) fresh (roughly a 1 to 4 ratio). Dried herbs taste best used in longer-cooking recipes; fresh herbs taste best in shorter-cooking ones.

Learn how to buy, store, and freeze herbs and spices in our information on pages 8 and 9. Our two glossaries, pages 15 and 19, describe the herbs and spices we used in these recipes and suggest foods for which they are best suited.

Did you know that ginger and cinnamon can increase circulation and peppermint can

relieve headaches? Or that marjoram soothes insect bites and stings, garlic was used to ward off the Plague, and mint eases indigestion? These culinary favourites not only enrich our food but can also help to keep us healthy.

So whether your choice is hot and spicy or gently herbed foods, you'll find no shortage of recipe ideas in this book. Pique your senses with an aromatic addition to dinner or an alluring new taste for dessert. Soon you'll find that *Herbs & Spices* is an indispensable guide to your mealtime pleasure. Savour the flavour!

Jean Paré

Each recipe has been analyzed using the most up-to-date version of the Canadian Nutrient File from Health Canada, which is based on the United States Department of Agriculture (USDA) Nutrient Data Base. If more than one ingredient is listed (such as "hard margarine or butter"), or a range is given (1 – 2 tsp., 5 – 10 mL) then the first ingredient or amount is used in the analysis. Where an ingredient reads "sprinkle," "optional," or "for garnish," it is not included as part of the nutrition information. Milk, unless stated otherwise, is 1% and cooking oil, unless stated otherwise, is canola.

Margaret Ng, B.Sc. (Hon), M.A.
Registered Dietitian

What's An Herb? What's A Spice?

Anything with a leaf and a mild flavour that's grown in a temperate climate is an herb. Everything else (including seeds, bark, berries and underground roots and shoots) that has a stronger flavour and grows in tropical climates is considered a spice.

HERBS

Which Is Best—Fresh or Dried?

Dried herbs are more convenient and less costly than fresh herbs but are best used with longer cooking dishes (such as stews, sauces and chilies) because they lend moisture to the herbs. When using quicker-cooking techniques (such as stir-frying, sautéing or broiling), choose fresh herbs because they'll retain their moisture, preserving the herb's vibrant taste and colour. Fresh herbs also impart a truer flavour in salads and sandwich fillings because, although no heat is applied, the dressing helps keep them moist.

You can buy both fresh and dried herbs from your local grocery store or, if you prefer, you can grow your own fresh herbs in a kitchen herb garden. Many local farmers' markets are also a good source of fresh herbs.

Storing Herbs

Store dried herbs in small glass jars with airtight seals or screw tops or in opaque jars made either of china or metal in a cool, dark cupboard away from the heat of the stove.

Store fresh herbs in the refrigerator. Don't wash them until you're ready to use them because they quickly rot. If herbs are wet, shake off excess moisture, then wrap in paper towels or keep at room temperature until the leaves dry.

To dry fresh herbs for longer storage, several methods can be used:

1) Air - Remove all soil and roots, then wash and gently dry. Hang in bunches upside down in a paper bag with air holes in a well-ventilated area.

2) Microwave - This is the best way to preserve an herb's colour. Spread between layers of paper towel and heat on high (100%) for about 2 minutes, checking every 30 seconds and removing herbs as they dry. Leave on counter to cool and dry completely before storing.

3) Oven - Spread herbs on baking sheet with sides in a thin layer. Bake at lowest heat in oven, without stirring, until leaves are dry and crispy. Do not overdry.

Freezing Fresh Herbs

Wash and finely chop herbs. Pack into plastic ice cube trays. Fill trays with water and freeze. Remove cubes and store in labelled freezer bags for up to 6 months. Drop a cube, as needed, into your latest culinary concoction.

SPICES

Buying and Grinding Spices

Choose whole seeds, berries, buds and bark, because they retain their flavour longer than powdered spices and can be easily ground as needed.

Crush or grind whole spices to release their flavour and aroma. Grind in small quantities, not more than 1 tbsp. (15 mL) at a time, and only as much as you'll need. Don't grind or crush more than 2 days before using. An electric coffee grinder works well, but purchase one solely for this use, as your usual coffee grinder will taint your spice flavours and the spices will taint your coffee!

Storing Spices

Keep freshly ground spices chilled rather than storing them at room temperature. To keep them fresh longer, grind and make them into a paste by adding just a bit of olive oil. Store in small sealed containers or freeze for up to 6 months.

Keep ground spices in small glass jars with airtight seals in a cool, dark cupboard. Opaque jars made either of china or metal don't need to be stored in a dark place but should still be kept in a cool (but not chilled) place.

About Marinades

Marinades can tenderize and add distinct flavour to meat before cooking. Generally 1/2 cup (125 mL) of marinade will be sufficient for each 1 lb. (454 g) of meat or fish.

Beef, pork and poultry are best marinated for at least 6 hours or overnight. Fish and seafood should marinate no longer than 30 minutes to avoid fish becoming mushy. Always marinate meats and fish in the refrigerator.

Discard marinade that has come in contact with uncooked meat or seafood. However, if desired, marinade can be boiled for at least 5 minutes to kill any bacteria from uncooked meat. It may then be used to baste meat during grilling or served as a sauce with cooked meat.

TO MARINATE

Method 1: Place your choice of meat or seafood in resealable freezer bag. Pour marinade over meat. Seal bag. Turn carefully until coated. Marinate in refrigerator for recommended amount of time. Use this method with 1 cup (250 mL) of marinade or less.

Method 2: Place your choice of meat or seafood in large non-metallic bowl. Pour marinade over meat. Stir until coated. Cover bowl with plastic wrap. Marinate in refrigerator for recommended amount of time.

Sweet Basil Marinade

Best with chicken or white fish such as halibut.

Dijon mustard (with whole seeds)	1/4 cup	60 mL
Brown sugar, packed	1/4 cup	60 mL
Chopped fresh basil (or 1 tbsp., 15 mL, dried)	1/4 cup	60 mL
Olive (or cooking) oil	3 tbsp.	50 mL
Apple cider vinegar	3 tbsp.	50 mL
Dry mustard	1 tsp.	5 mL

Process all 6 ingredients in blender or food processor until smooth. Makes 3/4 cup (175 mL).

1 tbsp. (15 mL): 53 Calories; 3.7 g Total Fat (2.5 g Mono, 0.5 g Poly, 0.5 g Sat); 0 mg Cholesterol; 5 g Carbohydrate; trace Fibre; 0 g Protein; 70 mg Sodium

Coconut Curry Marinade

A tropical taste—great with strips of pork loin or chicken breast fillets.
Not recommended for red meat.

Coconut milk (or reconstituted from powder)	2/3 cup	150 mL
Curry powder	2 tsp.	10 mL
Lime (or lemon) juice	2 tsp.	10 mL
Garlic clove, minced (or 1/4 tsp.,1 mL, powder)	1	1
Granulated sugar	1 tsp.	5 mL
Dried crushed chilies	1 tsp.	5 mL

Measure all 6 ingredients into small bowl. Stir well. Makes 3/4 cup (175 mL).

1 tbsp. (15 mL): 29 Calories; 2.8 g Total Fat (0.1 g Mono, 0 g Poly, 2.4 g Sat); 0 mg Cholesterol; 1 g Carbohydrate; trace Fibre; 0 g Protein; 4 mg Sodium

---

Red Wine Marinade

Full-flavoured marinade with a hint of sweetness. Goes well with lamb, beef and buffalo.

Dry red wine	1/2 cup	125 mL
Olive (or cooking) oil	3 tbsp.	50 mL
Chopped fresh parsley	1/4 cup	60 mL
Barbecue Spice Mix, page 13	1 1/2 tbsp.	25 mL
Granulated sugar	1 tbsp.	15 mL
Garlic cloves, minced (or 1/2 tsp., 2 mL, powder)	2	2

Measure all 6 ingredients into small bowl. Stir well. Makes 3/4 cup (175 mL).

1 tbsp. (15 mL): 48 Calories; 3.4 g Total Fat (2.4 g Mono, 0.3 g Poly, 0.5 g Sat); 0 mg Cholesterol; 3 g Carbohydrate; trace Fibre; 0 g Protein; 70 mg Sodium

Sun-Dried Tomato Pesto

Thick and flavourful with a deep, earthy red colour. Spread on steaks or chicken just before cooking is complete.

Jar of sun-dried tomatoes in oil (not drained)	8 1/2 oz.	251 mL
Fresh basil, packed (or 1 tbsp., 15 mL, dried)	1/4 cup	60 mL
Fresh parsley, packed (or 1 tbsp., 15 mL, flakes)	1/4 cup	60 mL
Pine nuts, toasted (see Tip, page 33)	1/4 cup	60 mL
Grated Parmesan cheese	1/4 cup	60 mL
Garlic cloves, minced (or 1/2 tsp., 2 mL, powder)	2	2

Process all 6 ingredients in blender or food processor until smooth. Makes 1 1/4 cups (300 mL).

1 tbsp. (15 mL): 29 Calories; 2.2 g Total Fat (1 g Mono, 0.6 g Poly, 0.5 g Sat); 1 mg Cholesterol; 2 g Carbohydrate; trace Fibre; 1 g Protein; 39 mg Sodium

TOMATO PESTO PASTA: Add 2 tbsp. (30 mL) pesto to 2 cups (500 mL) hot cooked pasta. Toss until coated. Sprinkle with Parmesan cheese.

TOMATO PESTO DRESSING: Combine pesto with equal amount of olive (or cooking) oil and just a pinch of salt. Add to your favourite green salad. Toss.

TOMATO PESTO CROSTINI: Spread pesto on 1 side of toasted baguette slices. Sprinkle with grated Parmesan cheese. Broil. Serve as an appetizer or accompaniment to soup or salad.

Basil Pesto

Great as a marinade for chicken. Classic flavours of basil and garlic are perfect on pasta too!

Fresh basil, packed	2 cups	500 mL
Pine nuts, toasted (see Tip, page 33)	1/4 cup	60 mL
Grated Parmesan cheese	1/4 cup	60 mL
Olive (or cooking) oil	1/4 cup	60 mL
Garlic clove, minced (or 1/4 tsp., 1 mL, powder)	1	1
Salt	1/4 tsp.	1 mL
Pepper, just a pinch		
Olive (or cooking) oil	1/4 cup	60 mL

Process first 7 ingredients in blender or food processor until finely chopped.

With motor running, slowly add second amount of olive oil in steady stream through hole in lid or feed chute until mixture is thick and grainy. Makes about 1 1/3 cups (325 mL).

1 tbsp. (15 mL): 62 Calories; 6.5 g Total Fat (4.3 g Mono, 0.9 g Poly, 1.1 g Sat); 1 mg Cholesterol; 1 g Carbohydrate; trace Fibre; 1 g Protein; 49 mg Sodium

Barbecue Spice Mix

Rub or sprinkle on chicken, pork or beef while grilling. Nicely balanced BBQ flavour.

Celery seed	2 tsp.	10 mL
Dried marjoram (or dried whole oregano)	2 tsp.	10 mL
Brown sugar, packed	2 tsp.	10 mL
Paprika	1 tsp.	5 mL
Ground nutmeg	1 tsp.	5 mL
Chili powder	1 tsp.	5 mL
Garlic powder	1 tsp.	5 mL
Salt	1 tsp.	5 mL
Pepper	1 tsp.	5 mL

Measure all 9 ingredients into small bowl. Stir well. Makes 1/4 cup (60 mL).

1/4 tsp. (1 mL): 2 Calories; 0.1 g Total Fat (0 g Mono, 0 g Poly, 0 g Sat); 0 mg Cholesterol; 0 g Carbohydrate; trace Fibre; 0 g Protein; 48 mg Sodium

Jean's Jazz

Keep handy in shaker. Try in Jazzy Snack Mix, page 26, Dill Cucumber Dip, page 29, and Jazz 'N' Roll Chicken, page 76.

Salt	1/4 cup	60 mL
Paprika	1/4 cup	60 mL
Pepper	3 tbsp.	50 mL
Dried basil	1 tbsp.	15 mL
Garlic powder	2 tsp.	10 mL
Dried thyme	2 tsp.	10 mL
Dried whole oregano	1 1/2 tsp.	7 mL
Curry powder	1 tsp.	5 mL
Dried marjoram	1 tsp.	5 mL
Cayenne pepper	1 tsp.	5 mL
Celery salt	1 tsp.	5 mL

Process all 11 ingredients in blender or food processor until well combined. Makes about 3/4 cup (175 mL).

1/4 tsp. (1 mL): 1 Calorie; 0 g Total Fat (0 g Mono, 0 g Poly, 0 g Sat); 0 mg Cholesterol; 0 g Carbohydrate; trace Fibre; 0 g Protein; 196 mg Sodium

Seasoned Salt

A good all-purpose seasoning. Use in place of store-bought seasoned salt.

Salt	3/4 cup	175 mL
Paprika	2 tbsp.	30 mL
Onion powder	1 tbsp.	15 mL
Garlic powder	1 tbsp.	15 mL
Pepper	1 tbsp.	15 mL
Celery seed	1 tsp.	5 mL
Dry mustard	1 tsp.	5 mL
Ground marjoram	1/2 tsp.	2 mL
Ground ginger	1/4 tsp.	1 mL
Cayenne pepper	1/4 tsp.	1 mL

Measure all 10 ingredients into small bowl. Stir well. Makes about 1 cup (250 mL).

1/4 tsp. (1 mL): 1 Calorie; 0 g Total Fat (0 g Mono, 0 g Poly, 0 g Sat); 0 mg Cholesterol; 0 g Carbohydrate; trace Fibre; 0 g Protein; 443 mg Sodium

Herbs Glossary

Basil (pictured on page 17): Has a licorice-spice flavour. When dried, flavour is like lemon and anise. Especially good with tomatoes, seafood, vegetables and venison, as well as in pasta dishes, pesto, salad dressings and soups.

Bay Leaf: Flavour is woodsy with traces of cinnamon. Use individual dried leaves in casseroles, marinades, rice dishes, soups and stews, and with roasts, seafood, venison and vegetables.

Chives (pictured on page 17): A slightly sweet, delicate onion flavour. Best used fresh but can be dried or frozen. Use with fish, soft cheeses and vegetables and in egg dishes, herb mixtures, salad dressings, salads and soups.

Cilantro (pictured on page 17): A distinct astringent flavour. Use fresh leaves in Mexican and Chinese cooking, biscuits, breads, pies, poultry stuffing, salads and soups and with roasts.

Curry Powder: A combination of up to 20 spices, herbs and seeds including cayenne pepper, cumin, coriander, ginger and turmeric. Use in East Indian cooking, with beef, lamb, poultry and vegetables. Also good in egg dishes, fruit dishes and rice dishes.

Dill (pictured on page 17): Has a sweet, full aroma. Stems, leaves (dill weed) and seeds can be fresh, dried or frozen. Use with fish and in breads, egg dishes, fish, pasta dishes, pickled cucumbers, soups and vegetables.

Lavender (pictured on page 17): Bitter, pungent flavour with a floral aroma. Use the dried flowers and leaves in salads or just the leaves to make an herbal tea. A water or milk infusion can be made to flavour other beverages and desserts.

Lemon Grass (pictured on page 17): A bulb with long, thin, green-grey leaves and a sour lemon flavour. Dried lemon grass is known as sereh—1 tsp. (5 mL) equals 1 lemon grass stalk. Use in Thai cooking, with poultry and seafood, and in marinades, salads and soups.

Marjoram (pictured on page 17): Smooth leaves with an oregano-like flavour but slightly sweeter. Delicious fresh but can be dried (or ground) or frozen. Use with beef, lamb and pork, and in fish sauces, pasta dishes, rice dishes, soups, stews and vegetables.

(continued on next page)

Mint (pictured on page 17): Best fresh. Use in Middle Eastern cooking, fruit dishes, vegetable salads and as a garnish.

Oregano (pictured on page 17): Strong, pungent flavour, similar to marjoram but not as sweet. Commonly used dried (or ground), but fresh is readily available. Use in Italian, Spanish and Mexican cooking, beans, cheese dishes, egg dishes, sauces, soups, tomato dishes and with meats.

Parsley (pictured on page 17): Good fresh, dried or frozen. Use in egg dishes, marinades, rice dishes, salads, sauces, soups and with potatoes.

Rosemary (pictured on page 17): Potent flavour and aroma. Retains flavour well when dried or frozen. Use in basting sauces, biscuits, breads, egg dishes, soups and with meats, poached fish and poultry.

Sage (pictured on page 17): Strong flavour, so use sparingly. Use fresh or dried in cheese dishes, dips, poultry stuffing and salads. Combine with fennel for fish, veal and sausage.

Savory (pictured on page 17): Winter savory has small, thin, aromatic leaves. Use with venison and pâtés. Summer savory is more delicate with a peppery flavour similar to marjoram or thyme. Use in egg dishes, rice dishes, salads and soups, and with fish, green beans, legumes, lentils, meats, poultry, rice dishes and squash.

Tarragon (pictured on page 17): Retains flavour well when dried or frozen. Use in salad dressing and with egg dishes, poached fish, pickles, preserves and vegetables.

Thyme (pictured on page 17): A sweet fragrance that should be used sparingly. Use in French cooking, with all meats and poultry, and in chowders, marinades, pasta dishes, rice dishes, sauces and vegetables (especially potatoes, mushrooms and tomatoes).

Herbs Glossary

Herbs

Basil

Chives

Cilantro

Dill

Lavender

Marjoram

Mint

Oregano

Parsley

Rosemary

Sage

Lemon Grass

Savory

Tarragon

Thyme

Spices

Star Anise

Caraway Seed

Cardamom Pod

Cayenne Pepper

Celery Seed

Cloves

Coriander

Cumin

Fennel

Mustard Seed

Saffron

Turmeric

Spices Glossary

Aniseed and **Star Anise** (pictured on page 18): A sweet licorice flavour with heat. The dominant flavour in Chinese five-spice powder. Use in baking, cocktails, soups and warm milk.

Caraway Seed (pictured on page 18): Nutty flavour. Enhance the distinct flavour by toasting the seeds. Use in German cooking, breads, cheese dishes, soups, and with cabbage and sauerkraut.

Cardamom Pod (pictured on page 18): A spicy-sweet flavour. Use in East Indian and Scandinavian cooking, curries, garam masala, pickling brine, pilaus, other spice mixtures and waffle batter.

Cayenne (KI-yen) **Pepper** (pictured on page 18): A pungent flavour that packs a lot of heat in a small amount. Use in breads, cheese dishes, chilies, chowders, cream cheese spreads, egg dishes, guacamole, salad dressings, salsa and sauces.

Celery Seed (pictured on page 18): Adds the flavour of celery to pickles, salads, salad dressings, soups and stews, as well as to tomato juice or Bloody Mary cocktails.

Chili Powder: Combination of chili peppers, cumin, garlic, oregano, and salt. Use in Mexican cooking, chilies and stews.

Chinese Five-Spice Powder: Blend of cloves, cumin, fennel, star anise and Szechuan peppercorns. Can be purchased at Asian specialty stores and larger grocery stores.

Cinnamon: A mild, lingering flavour. Use either as sticks or in ground form in beverages, breads, cookies, quick breads and pies.

Cloves (pictured on page 18): An aromatic spice with a potent taste. Use in beverages, chilies, baked beans, ham and pumpkin pie.

Coriander (pictured on page 18): Seeds of the cilantro (Chinese parsley) with a lemony sage flavour with added sweetness. Add to pickles and marinades. Use in cakes, apple pie, frying batters and fruit salads.

Cumin (KUH-min; KYOO-min) (pictured on page 18): Essential in curry and chili powders. Use in cheese spread, rice or couscous, chili beans or lentils, salad dressing or yogurt.

Dried Crushed Chilies: Dried chili peppers with a medium to hot heat. Use in sauces, soups or stir-fries. Pale green chilies are generally milder than small red ones.

Fennel (pictured on page 18): Has a sweet licorice flavour. Best fresh. Seeds and bulb are both used in cooking. Use in seafood and pork dishes, breads, cakes, pastries, sauces and soups.

(continued on next page)

Garlic: Tastes strongest when freshly cut or minced; mellows when baked, fried or stewed. Use in sauces, dressings, soups, stews, and dishes with meats, fish, poultry, tomato and green vegetables.

Ginger: A hot, sweet spice. The fresh form is gingerroot and it must be peeled, then sliced, chopped or finely grated. Ginger powder is a reasonable substitute but will produce quite a different flavour. Use in Asian cooking, beverages, breads, fruit salads, pies and custards, and with sweet potatoes or yams.

Mustard Seed (pictured on page 18): A spicy, almost sweet flavour. Use with meats (especially beef brisket or corned beef), fish, cabbage, green beans, and in pickling brine and cream sauces.

Nutmeg: Mace is the covering of the nutmeg seed and the two can be used interchangeably though mace is stronger. Most common form is ground. Use in cream sauces, soups, winter squash, sweet potatoes, carrots, parsnips and pies.

Paprika: Colourful, finely ground sweet red pepper pods. Flavour from mild to rich. Hungary produces the best variety. Use in potato dishes, poultry, stews, soups and salads.

Peppercorns: There are 3 varieties. Green peppercorns are mild, with a fresh flavour. Use with butter and in light sauces. Black peppercorns are dark brown to black with a rich and spicy flavour. White peppercorns have a hot flavour, with sometimes a hint of ginger. Peppercorns can be used whole or crushed. Use to season meat, salads, fruit, baking and side dishes.

Poppy Seeds: Nutty and sweet with a grainy texture. Use as topping for breads, rolls and cookies, sprinkled into noodles, some pork dishes, eggs, cheese and vegetables.

Saffron (pictured on page 18): Said to be the most expensive spice in the world, it is purchased in threads. Aromatic and golden-coloured: the deeper the colour, the better the quality. Use sparingly.

Sesame Seeds: Nutty and sweet. Black seeds are more flavourful and aromatic than white. Often toasted before using. Use as a garnish for breads, rolls, cookies and salads.

Turmeric (pictured on page 18): Has a bitter, pungent flavour and an intense colour. Used in East Indian cooking and provides the distinct colour in prepared mustard.

Vanilla Bean: Subtle, sweet taste and distinct aroma. Use in all kinds of baking, salads, ice cream and alcohol. Enhances the flavour of chocolate, too.

Spices Glossary

Moroccan Spice Rub

An aromatic combination of spices that goes well with pork, lamb or beef.
Use in Olive-Stuffed Chicken, page 77.

Ground cumin	1 tbsp.	15 mL
Ground coriander	1 tbsp.	15 mL
Ground ginger	1 tbsp.	15 mL
Chili powder	2 tsp.	10 mL
Granulated sugar	2 tsp.	10 mL
Salt	2 tsp.	10 mL
Ground cinnamon	1 tsp.	5 mL
Garlic powder	1 tsp.	5 mL

Measure all 8 ingredients into small bowl. Stir well. Makes about 1/3 cup (75 mL).

1/4 tsp. (1 mL): 2 Calories; 0 g Total Fat (0 g Mono, 0 g Poly, 0 g Sat); 0 mg Cholesterol;
0 g Carbohydrate; trace Fibre; 0 g Protein; 73 mg Sodium

Cajun Spice Mix

Sizzling Cajun flavour! Rub on lamb or beef or use for Cajun Garlic Shrimp,
page 91. Have on hand for grilling, casseroles, stews and stir-fries.

Paprika	2 tsp.	10 mL
Dried whole oregano	2 tsp.	10 mL
Pepper	1 tsp.	5 mL
Dry mustard	1 tsp.	5 mL
Cayenne pepper	1 tsp.	5 mL
Dried thyme (not ground)	1 tsp.	5 mL
Ground cumin	1/2 tsp.	2 mL
Garlic powder	1/2 tsp.	2 mL
Salt	1/2 tsp.	2 mL

Measure all 9 ingredients into small cup. Stir well. Makes about 3 tbsp. (50 mL).

1/4 tsp. (1 mL): 2 Calories; 0 g Total Fat (0 g Mono, 0 g Poly, 0 g Sat); 0 mg Cholesterol;
0 g Carbohydrate; trace Fibre; 0 g Protein; 33 mg Sodium

Beef Spring Rolls

A surprising infusion of Asian flavours. Garnish with chopped pistachios.

Cooking oil	2 tsp.	10 mL
Finely chopped onion	1/2 cup	125 mL
Ground ginger	1 tsp.	5 mL
Chili powder	1 tsp.	5 mL
Ground cinnamon	1 tsp.	5 mL
Ground cumin	1/2 tsp.	2 mL
Garlic cloves, minced (or 1/2 tsp., 2 mL, powder)	2	2
Pistachios, toasted (see Tip, page 33) and chopped	1/2 cup	125 mL
Currants	1/3 cup	75 mL
Liquid honey	1 tbsp.	15 mL
Salt	1/4 tsp.	1 mL
Lean ground beef	3/4 lb.	340 g
Water	1/3 cup	75 mL
All-purpose flour	1/3 cup	75 mL
Spring roll wrappers (6 inch, 15 cm, square)	44	44

Cooking oil, for deep-frying

Heat cooking oil in medium frying pan on medium. Add onion. Cook for 5 to 10 minutes, stirring often, until softened.

Add next 5 ingredients. Heat and stir for 1 to 2 minutes until fragrant. Transfer to large bowl. Cool slightly.

Add next 4 ingredients. Stir. Add beef. Mix well.

Stir water into flour in small cup until smooth. Work with spring roll wrappers 1 at a time. Keep remaining wrappers covered with damp tea towel to prevent drying. Place 1 wrapper diagonally on work surface. Place 1 tbsp. (15 mL) beef mixture on wrapper near bottom corner. Brush edges of wrapper with flour mixture. Fold bottom corner over filling. Fold side corners over filling. Roll up toward top corner to seal. Cover with damp tea towel. Repeat with remaining wrappers, beef mixture and flour mixture to make a total of 44 rolls.

(continued on next page)

Appetizers

Deep-fry spring rolls in batches in hot (375°F, 190°C) cooking oil for about 3 minutes until golden and beef is no longer pink. Remove to paper towels to drain. Makes 44 rolls.

1 roll: 172 Calories; 7.3 g Total Fat (4 g Mono, 1.8 g Poly, 1 g Sat); 7 mg Cholesterol; 21 g Carbohydrate; trace Fibre; 5 g Protein; 203 mg Sodium

Pictured on page 90.

Marinated Feta

Feta and red pepper infused with savoury herbs and spices.

Dried whole oregano	1 tbsp.	15 mL
Cumin seed	1 tbsp.	15 mL
Sprigs of fresh rosemary (about 1 1/2 inch, 3.8 cm, length)	3	3
Pepper	2 tsp.	10 mL
Red medium peppers, seeds and ribs removed, quartered (see Note)	2	2
Feta cheese, cut into 3/4 inch (2 cm) cubes	12 oz.	340 g
Olive (or cooking) oil	1/2 cup	125 mL

Combine first 4 ingredients in large bowl.

Arrange peppers, skin-side up, on ungreased baking sheet. Broil 5 inches (12.5 cm) from heat for about 10 minutes until skins are blackened and blistered. Remove to small bowl. Cover with plastic wrap. Let sweat for about 15 minutes until cool enough to handle. Peel and discard skins. Cut into 1/3 inch (1 cm) thick strips. Add to oregano mixture.

Add feta cheese and olive oil. Stir gently until coated. Transfer to airtight container. Marinate in refrigerator for at least 3 days, but no longer than 7 days, to blend flavours. Drain and discard marinade. Makes 2 cups (500 mL) marinated feta. Serves 12.

1 serving: 129 Calories; 11.2 g Total Fat (4.9 g Mono, 0.6 g Poly, 5 g Sat); 26 mg Cholesterol; 3 g Carbohydrate; trace Fibre; 4 g Protein; 328 mg Sodium

Pictured on page 35.

Note: Prepared roasted red peppers are available in jars in most grocery stores. Drain well. Use in place of fresh, roasted red peppers.

Twisted Chopsticks

A crisp and flaky twist to the familiar bread stick.
Great addition to a plate of Asian-style appetizers.

Package of frozen puff pastry, thawed according to package directions	14 oz.	397 g
Egg yolk (large)	1	1
Oyster sauce	2 tbsp.	30 mL
Chinese five-spice powder	1 tsp.	5 mL
Sesame seeds	2 tbsp.	30 mL
Coarse salt (such as sea salt)	2 tsp.	10 mL
Chinese five-spice powder	1 tsp.	5 mL
Sesame seeds	1 tbsp.	15 mL
Egg white (large)	1	1
Milk	1 tbsp.	15 mL

Roll out 1/2 of pastry (1 square) on lightly floured surface to 7 x 12 inch (18 x 30 cm) rectangle. Keep remaining 1/2 of pastry (1 square) chilled.

Beat egg yolk, oyster sauce and first amount of five-spice powder in small bowl until blended. Brush about 1/2 of egg yolk mixture evenly over pastry.

Sprinkle with 1 tbsp. (15 mL) of first amount of sesame seeds. Fold pastry in half, crosswise, into 6 x 7 inch (15 x 18 cm) rectangle. Press down lightly. Place on ungreased baking sheet. Cover with plastic wrap. Repeat with remaining pastry, egg yolk mixture and sesame seeds. Chill for 1 1/2 hours. Line 2 separate ungreased baking sheets with parchment (not waxed) paper. Cut each pastry rectangle into twelve 1/2 x 7 inch (12 mm x 18 cm) strips, using pizza cutter or knife, for a total of 24 strips. Twist each strip several times. Place twists, about 2 inches (5 cm) apart, on baking sheets. Cover with plastic wrap. Chill for 30 minutes.

Combine coarse salt and second amounts of five-spice powder and sesame seeds in small cup.

Beat egg white and milk in separate small cup. Brush top of each twist with egg white mixture. Sprinkle with salt mixture. Bake in 400°F (205°C) oven for about 15 minutes until golden brown and crisp. Let stand on baking sheets for 5 minutes before removing to wire racks to cool. Makes 24 bread sticks.

1 bread stick: 103 Calories; 7.1 g Total Fat (1.7 g Mono, 3.9 g Poly, 1.1 g Sat); 9 mg Cholesterol; 8 g Carbohydrate; trace Fibre; 2 g Protein; 348 mg Sodium

Pictured on page 90.

Minty Sweet Chicken Skewers

Glistening with tasty marinade. Great with Roasted Curry Dip, page 27.

Apricot jam	1/3 cup	75 mL
Warm water	3 tbsp.	50 mL
Chopped fresh cilantro or parsley (or 2 1/4 tsp., 11 mL, dried)	3 tbsp.	50 mL
Chopped fresh mint leaves (or 1 1/2 tsp., 7 mL, dried)	2 tbsp.	30 mL
Ground cumin	1 tsp.	5 mL
Paprika	1 tsp.	5 mL
Finely grated lime zest	1 tsp.	5 mL
Sesame oil, for flavour	1 tsp.	5 mL
Garlic cloves, minced (or 1/2 tsp., 2 mL, powder)	2	2
Boneless, skinless chicken breast halves (4 – 6 oz., 113 – 170 g, each), cut into 1/2 inch (12 mm) thick strips (see Tip, below)	6	6
Bamboo skewers (8 inch, 20 cm, length), soaked in water for 10 minutes	16	16

Measure first 9 ingredients into large bowl. Stir.

Add chicken. Stir until coated. Cover. Marinate in refrigerator for at least 3 hours, stirring several times. Drain and discard marinade.

Thread chicken, accordion-style, onto skewers. Preheat electric grill for 5 minutes or gas barbecue to medium. Cook chicken on greased grill (or broil in oven) for about 10 minutes, turning several times, until chicken is tender and no longer pink. Makes 16 skewers.

1 skewer: 70 Calories; 1.2 g Total Fat (0.3 g Mono, 0.3 g Poly, 0.3 g Sat); 31 mg Cholesterol; 2 g Carbohydrate; trace Fibre; 12 g Protein; 2 mg Sodium

 To slice meat easily, place in freezer for about 30 minutes until just beginning to freeze. If using from frozen state, partially thaw before slicing.

Jazzy Snack Mix

Savoury and satisfying. A nice change from chips or popcorn.

Hard margarine (or butter), melted	1/2 cup	125 mL
Worcestershire sauce	2 tbsp.	30 mL
Jean's Jazz, page 14	2 tbsp.	30 mL
"O"-shaped toasted oat cereal (such as Cheerios)	2 cups	500 mL
Whole wheat squares cereal (such as Shreddies)	2 cups	500 mL
Oat squares cereal (such as Life)	2 cups	500 mL
Cheese-flavoured, fish-shaped crackers	1 cup	250 mL
Chow mein noodles	1 cup	250 mL
Pretzels (snack-size)	1 cup	250 mL
Unsalted peanuts	1/2 cup	125 mL

Measure first 3 ingredients into small bowl. Stir.

Combine remaining 7 ingredients in large bowl. Drizzle with margarine mixture. Toss until coated. Spread on ungreased baking sheet. Bake in 250°F (120°C) oven for about 45 minutes, stirring every 15 minutes, until crisp and dry. Makes 10 cups (2.5 L).

1 cup (250 mL): 309 Calories; 17.8 g Total Fat (9.3 g Mono, 3.5 g Poly, 3.4 g Sat); 1 mg Cholesterol; 33 g Carbohydrate; 3 g Fibre; 7 g Protein; 974 mg Sodium

Pictured on page 35.

Herbed Cheese Spread

One taste and you'll be hooked! Delicious on crackers or crusty bread.

Block of cream cheese, cut up and softened	8 oz.	250 g
Finely chopped fresh parsley	3 tbsp.	50 mL
Chopped fresh chives	3 tbsp.	50 mL
Pepper	1 tsp.	5 mL

(continued on next page)

Appetizers

Sweet (or regular) chili sauce	2 tbsp.	30 mL
Soy sauce	1 tbsp.	15 mL
Finely chopped fresh parsley, for garnish	1 tsp.	5 mL
Chopped fresh chives, for garnish	1 tsp.	5 mL

Beat cream cheese in medium bowl until smooth.

Combine parsley, chives and pepper in small cup. Add to cream cheese. Beat well.

Add chili sauce and soy sauce to cream cheese mixture. Beat well. Transfer to serving bowl. Cover. Chill for at least 2 hours to blend flavours.

Garnish with parsley and chives. Makes about 1 1/4 cups (300 mL).

1 tbsp. (15 mL): 46 Calories; 4.3 g Total Fat (1.2 g Mono, 0.2 g Poly, 2.7 g Sat); 14 mg Cholesterol; 1 g Carbohydrate; trace Fibre; 1 g Protein; 112 mg Sodium

Pictured on page 35.

Roasted Curry Dip

Serve with fresh vegetables, bread or crackers.
Great with Minty Sweet Chicken Skewers, page 25.

Curry powder	1 tbsp.	15 mL
Ranch dressing	1 cup	250 mL

Heat and stir curry powder in small frying pan on medium-low for about 5 minutes until fragrant. Transfer to small bowl. Let stand until cool.

Add ranch dressing. Stir well. Cover. Chill for at least 30 minutes to blend flavours. Makes 1 cup (250 mL).

2 tbsp. (30 mL): 156 Calories; 15.9 g Total Fat (8.8 g Mono, 5.3 g Poly, 1.1 g Sat); 6 mg Cholesterol; 4 g Carbohydrate; trace Fibre; 1 g Protein; 270 mg Sodium

Pictured on page 35.

ROASTED CURRY SOUR CREAM: Substitute 1 cup (250 mL) sour cream for ranch dressing. Serve on baked potatoes or as dip for Minted Beef Skewers, page 81.

ROASTED CURRY MAYONNAISE: Substitute 1 cup (250 mL) mayonnaise for ranch dressing. Use in chicken salad, egg salad, or spread on Chicken Burgers, page 75.

Baba Ganoush

Flavourful Middle Eastern dip. Serve with Minted Pita Chips, page 30.

Small eggplants, halved lengthwise	2	2
Salt	1 tsp.	5 mL
Fresh bread crumbs	1/4 cup	60 mL
Lemon juice	1 tbsp.	15 mL
Olive (or cooking) oil	1 tbsp.	15 mL
Garlic clove, minced (or 1/4 tsp., 1 mL, powder)	1	1
Ground cumin	1/2 tsp.	2 mL
Salt	1/4 tsp.	1 mL
Pepper	1/4 tsp.	1 mL
Paprika (optional)	1/8 tsp.	0.5 mL

Place eggplant halves, skin-side down, on greased baking sheet. Sprinkle with salt. Let stand for 20 minutes. Rinse. Pat dry. Place, skin-side down, on same baking sheet. Bake in 350°F (175°C) oven for 25 to 30 minutes until softened. Let stand for 10 minutes. Scoop out flesh into food processor. Discard skin.

Add next 7 ingredients. Pulse with on/off motion for 20 to 30 seconds until almost smooth. Transfer to serving bowl. Cover. Chill for at least 3 hours to blend flavours.

Sprinkle with paprika. Makes 1 1/2 cups (375 mL).

2 tbsp. (30 mL): 7 Calories; 0.3 g Total Fat (0.3 g Mono, 0.1 g Poly, 0 g Sat); 0 mg Cholesterol; 1 g Carbohydrate; trace Fibre; 0 g Protein; 17 mg Sodium

Savoury Low-Fat Dip

Creamy, all-purpose dip. Perfect with raw vegetables.

Light sour cream	1/2 cup	125 mL
Ultra low-fat mayonnaise	1/2 cup	125 mL
Non-fat plain yogurt	1/2 cup	125 mL
Onion powder	1/2 tsp.	2 mL
Parsley flakes	1/2 tsp.	2 mL
Dried chives	1/2 tsp.	2 mL
Garlic powder	1/4 tsp.	1 mL
Paprika	1/8 tsp.	0.5 mL
Dill weed	1/8 tsp.	0.5 mL

Measure all 9 ingredients into small bowl. Stir well. Cover. Chill for at least 2 hours to blend flavours. Makes 1 1/3 cups (325 mL).

2 tbsp. (30 mL): 18 Calories; 0.8 g Total Fat (0.5 g Mono, 0.1 g Poly, 1 g Sat); 2 mg Cholesterol; 2 g Carbohydrate; trace Fibre; 1 g Protein; 82 mg Sodium

Dill Cucumber Dip

Dill and cucumber make this a refreshing dip!

Low-fat plain yogurt	2 cups	500 mL
Block of light cream cheese, softened	8 oz.	250 g
Low-fat salad dressing (or mayonnaise)	2 tbsp.	30 mL
Jean's Jazz, page 14 (or Seasoned Salt, page 14)	1/2 tsp.	2 mL
Finely diced English cucumber (with peel)	2 1/4 cups	550 mL
Chopped fresh dill (or 1 1/2 tsp., 7 mL, dill weed)	2 tbsp.	30 mL

Beat first 4 ingredients in medium bowl until smooth.

Fold in cucumber and dill. Cover. Chill for at least 2 hours to blend flavours. Makes about 4 cups (1 L).

1/3 cup (75 mL): 84 Calories; 5.4 g Total Fat (1.8 g Mono, 0.4 g Poly, 2.8 g Sat); 16 mg Cholesterol; 5 g Carbohydrate; trace Fibre; 4 g Protein; 228 mg Sodium

Bruschetta

Fresh tomatoes and garden fresh basil make this extra good!
Serve immediately while toasts are crisp.

Roma (plum) tomatoes, seeds removed, chopped	6	6
Grated Parmesan cheese	3 tbsp.	50 mL
Finely shredded fresh basil	2 tbsp.	30 mL
Olive (or cooking) oil	1 tbsp.	15 mL
Balsamic vinegar	2 tsp.	10 mL
Garlic clove, minced (or 1/4 tsp., 1 mL, powder)	1	1
Salt	1/4 tsp.	1 mL
Pepper, sprinkle		
Slices of crusty bread (such as baguette or ciabatta), 1/3 inch (1 cm) thick	10	10

Measure first 8 ingredients into medium bowl. Stir well. Cover. Chill for at least 30 minutes to blend flavours.

Arrange bread slices on ungreased baking sheet. Bake in 375°F (190°C) oven for 5 minutes. Turn over. Bake for 3 to 5 minutes until just golden. Cool. Spoon 3 tbsp. (50 mL) tomato mixture on each bread slice. Serve immediately. Makes 10 bruschetta.

1 bruschetta: 75 Calories; 2.6 g Total Fat (1.4 g Mono, 0.3 g Poly, 0.7 g Sat); 2 mg Cholesterol; 11 g Carbohydrate; 1 g Fibre; 3 g Protein; 187 mg Sodium

Minted Pita Chips

A delicious change from ordinary chips.
Excellent as a dipper with Baba Ganoush, page 28.

Finely chopped fresh mint leaves (or 1 1/2 tsp., 7 mL, dried)	2 tbsp.	30 mL
Olive (or cooking) oil	2 tbsp.	30 mL
Sesame seeds, toasted (see Tip, page 33)	2 tsp.	10 mL
Poppy seeds	2 tsp.	10 mL
Salt	1/8 tsp.	0.5 mL
Pita breads (7 inch, 18 cm, diameter)	3	3

(continued on next page)

Appetizers

Measure first 5 ingredients into small bowl. Stir.

Carefully split pita breads to make 6 rounds. Place inside-up on greased baking sheet. Divide and brush mint mixture over top of each. Bake in 350°F (175°C) oven for about 10 minutes until crisp and golden. Break into 2 to 3 inch (5 to 7.5 cm) pieces. Makes about 50 pita chips.

3 pita chips: 48 Calories; 2.1 g Total Fat (1.3 g Mono, 0.4 g Poly, 0.3 g Sat); 0 mg Cholesterol; 6 g Carbohydrate; trace Fibre; 1 g Protein; 77 mg Sodium

Spiced Peach Cooler

A tasty, make-ahead drink. Great for a backyard barbecue.

Apple juice	3 cups	750 mL
Granulated sugar	1 1/2 cups	375 mL
Ground mace	1/2 tsp.	2 mL
Whole cloves	9	9
Cinnamon sticks (4 inches, 10 cm, each)	2	2
Fresh peaches, peeled (see Tip, page 120) and pitted	6	6
Lemon juice	1/2 cup	125 mL
Crushed ice		
Club soda, chilled		
Lemon wedges, for garnish		

Measure first 5 ingredients into medium saucepan. Stir. Bring to a boil on medium. Reduce heat to medium-low. Cover. Simmer for 5 minutes. Remove from heat. Cool. Strain through sieve into large pitcher. Discard solids.

Process peaches in blender or food processor until smooth. Add to apple juice mixture.

Add lemon juice. Stir. Cover. Chill until ready to serve. Makes 8 cups (2 L) peach mixture.

Fill 16 small glasses 2/3 full with crushed ice. Pour 1/2 cup (125 mL) peach mixture into each. Top with club soda. Stir. Garnish each with lemon wedge. Serves 16.

1 serving: 116 Calories; 0.1 g Total Fat (0 g Mono, 0 g Poly, 0 g Sat); 0 mg Cholesterol; 30 g Carbohydrate; 1 g Fibre; 0 g Protein; 2 mg Sodium

Pictured on page 36.

Saffron Lassi

Saffron is made from the stigmas of crocuses and is the world's most expensive spice. A little goes a long way and it's well worth trying in this delicious beverage.

Saffron threads (see Glossary, page 20)	1/4 tsp.	1 mL
Boiling water	2 tbsp.	30 mL
Plain yogurt	2 cups	500 mL
Ice water	1 cup	250 mL
Granulated sugar	3 – 4 tbsp.	50 – 60 mL
Ground cinnamon	1/4 tsp.	1 mL
Ground cardamom	1/4 tsp.	1 mL
Ice cubes	12	12

Combine saffron and boiling water in small bowl. Let stand for 5 minutes. Stir. Pour into blender.

Add next 5 ingredients. Process for about 5 seconds until just blended.

Process, adding ice cubes 1 at a time through hole in lid, until smooth. Makes 4 2/3 cups (1.15 L). Serves 4.

1 serving: 102 Calories; 1.7 g Total Fat (0.5 g Mono, 0.1 g Poly, 1.1 g Sat); 7 mg Cholesterol; 16 g Carbohydrate; trace Fibre; 6 g Protein; 78 mg Sodium

Pictured on page 143.

Banana Cinnamon Smoothie

Thick, creamy and spicy. Delicious as a quick and easy smoothie for breakfast.

Medium ripe banana, frozen	1	1
Milk	1 cup	250 mL
Plain yogurt	1/3 cup	75 mL
Maple (or maple-flavoured) syrup	2 tbsp.	30 mL
Ground cinnamon	1/4 tsp.	1 mL
Ice cube	1	1

Process all 6 ingredients in blender until smooth. Makes 2 1/2 cups (625 mL). Serves 2.

1 serving: 224 Calories; 1.9 g Total Fat (0.5 g Mono, 0.1 g Poly, 1.1 g Sat); 6 mg Cholesterol; 48 g Carbohydrate; 1 g Fibre; 6 g Protein; 80 mg Sodium

Almond Lassi

A popular drink in India, lassi (LAH-see) resembles a milkshake. An excellent accompaniment to a spicy meal. Cool, refreshing and gently sweet.

Plain yogurt	2/3 cup	150 mL
Whole almonds, toasted (see Tip, below)	1/3 cup	75 mL
Almond-flavoured liqueur (such as Amaretto), or 1/4 tsp. (1 mL) almond flavouring	2 tbsp.	30 mL
Milk	2 cups	500 mL
Liquid honey	3 tbsp.	50 mL
Ground nutmeg	1/4 tsp.	1 mL
Ground cardamom (optional)	1/8 tsp.	0.5 mL
Ice cubes	8	8

Process yogurt, almonds and liqueur in blender until almonds are finely chopped.

Add next 4 ingredients. Process until smooth.

Process, adding ice cubes 1 at a time through hole in lid, until smooth. Makes about 5 1/4 cups (1.3 L). Serves 4.

1 serving: 178 Calories; 6.4 g Total Fat (3.5 g Mono, 1.1 g Poly, 1.5 g Sat); 6 mg Cholesterol; 22 g Carbohydrate; 1 g Fibre; 7 g Protein; 74 mg Sodium

 tip

To toast seeds, nuts or coconut, spread evenly in ungreased shallow pan. Bake in 350°F (175°C) oven for 5 to 10 minutes, stirring or shaking often, until desired doneness.

Special Spiced Coffee

Lightly sweetened, aromatic coffee garnished with perfectly spiced whipped cream topping. The perfect end to an elegant meal.

Whipping cream	1 cup	250 mL
Brown sugar, packed	1 tbsp.	15 mL
Ground cinnamon	3/4 tsp.	4 mL
Vanilla	1/2 tsp.	2 mL
Ground ginger	1/4 tsp.	1 mL
Ground nutmeg	1/4 tsp.	1 mL
Ground cardamom	1/8 tsp.	0.5 mL
Hot strong prepared coffee	4 1/2 cups	1.1 L
Coffee-flavoured liqueur (such as Kahlúa)	6 tbsp.	100 mL
Brown sugar, packed	2 tbsp.	30 mL

Beat first 7 ingredients in small bowl until stiff peaks form. Chill until ready to serve. Makes about 2 cups (500 mL) whipped cream mixture.

Pour hot coffee into heatproof 2 quart (2 L) pitcher. Add liqueur and second amount of brown sugar. Stir until sugar is dissolved. Pour into 6 large mugs. Top each with dollop of whipped cream mixture. Serves 6.

1 serving: 218 Calories; 13.6 g Total Fat (4 g Mono, 0.4 g Poly, 8.5 g Sat); 49 mg Cholesterol; 16 g Carbohydrate; trace Fibre; 1 g Protein; 27 mg Sodium

Pictured on page 144.

1. Jazzy Snack Mix, page 26
2. Marinated Feta, page 23
3. Roasted Curry Dip, page 27
4. Herbed Cheese Spread, page 26

Props Courtesy Of: Danesco Inc.
Klass Works

Cinn-Anise Iced Coffee

Star anise adds a unique touch to chilled coffee and cream. Strong and spicy.

Water	1 1/2 cups	375 mL
Ground dark-roasted coffee beans	1/4 cup	60 mL
Granulated sugar	2 – 3 tsp.	10 – 15 mL
Cinnamon stick (4 inches, 10 cm)	1	1
Star anise	1	1
Whipped cream (or frozen whipped topping, thawed), for garnish	1/4 cup	60 mL
Coarse brown sugar (such as Sugar in the Raw), for garnish	2 tsp.	10 mL

Measure first 5 ingredients into medium saucepan. Stir. Bring to a boil on medium-high. Reduce heat to medium-low. Simmer, uncovered, for 3 minutes. Remove from heat. Transfer to small heatproof bowl. Cover. Chill for 2 hours. Strain through fine sieve into 2 cup (500 mL) liquid measure or small pitcher. Discard solids. Chill for about 1 hour until cold. Makes 1 1/3 cups (325 mL).

Pour into 2 small glasses. Top with whipped cream. Sprinkle with brown sugar. Serves 2.

1 serving: 24 Calories; 0 g Total Fat (0 g Mono, 0 g Poly, 0 g Sat); 0 mg Cholesterol; 6 g Carbohydrate; 0 g Fibre; 0 g Protein; 1 mg Sodium

Pictured on page 36.

1. Spiced Peach Cooler, page 31
2. Lavender Lemonade, page 38
3. Cinn-Anise Iced Coffee, above

Props Courtesy Of: Lavender Harvest Farms
Stokes

Spiced Apple Beverage

Warm, fragrant and soothing. Perfect on a chilly winter evening.

Apple juice	4 cups	1 L
Star anise	2	2
Cinnamon sticks (4 inches, 10 cm, each)	2	2
Strip of orange peel (3/4 x 3 inches, 2 x 7.5 cm)	1	1
Whole cloves	6	6

Combine all 5 ingredients in medium saucepan. Bring to a boil on medium. Reduce heat to medium-low. Cover. Simmer for about 30 minutes, stirring occasionally, until fragrant. Strain through sieve. Discard solids. Makes 4 cups (1 L).

1 cup (250 mL): 123 Calories; 0.3 g Total Fat (0 g Mono, 0.1 g Poly, 0.1 g Sat); 0 mg Cholesterol; 31 g Carbohydrate; trace Fibre; 0 g Protein; 8 mg Sodium

SPICED PEAR BEVERAGE: Substitute same amount of pear juice for apple juice.

Lavender Lemonade

Subtle lavender flavour adds a special touch to sweet lemonade.

Water	2 1/2 cups	625 mL
Granulated sugar	1 1/2 cups	375 mL
Fresh lavender leaves	2 tbsp.	30 mL
Lemon juice	3/4 cup	175 mL
Vodka (optional)	3 oz.	85 mL

Crushed ice
Lemon slices, for garnish
Fresh lavender sprigs or flowers, for garnish

(continued on next page)

Beverages

Combine water and sugar in medium saucepan. Bring to a boil on medium. Reduce heat to medium-low. Simmer, uncovered, for 5 minutes, stirring occasionally.

Add lavender. Stir. Remove from heat. Let stand for 15 minutes. Strain through sieve. Discard solids. Transfer to heatproof pitcher.

Add lemon juice. Stir. Chill for at least 4 hours.

Add vodka. Stir. Makes about 3 cups (750 mL) lemonade.

Serve over crushed ice. Garnish with lemon slices and lavender. Serves 4.

1 serving: 425 Calories; 0 g Total Fat (0 g Mono, 0 g Poly, 0 g Sat); 0 mg Cholesterol; 111 g Carbohydrate; trace Fibre; 0 g Protein; 2 mg Sodium

Pictured on page 36.

Mulled Cognac Wine

Strong, spiced wine. Wonderfully warm beverage for a chilly autumn or winter day.

Water	1 1/2 cups	375 mL
Brown sugar, packed	3 tbsp.	50 mL
Cinnamon sticks (4 inches, 10 cm, each)	2	2
Whole cloves	6	6
Dry red wine	3 cups	750 mL
Cognac	3 tbsp.	50 mL
Orange slices, 1/4 inch (6 mm) thick	6	6

Measure first 4 ingredients into large saucepan. Heat and stir on medium for about 5 minutes until sugar is dissolved. Reduce heat to medium-low. Simmer, uncovered, for 5 minutes. Remove from heat. Let stand for 1 hour.

Add wine, cognac and orange slices. Heat and stir on medium-high until hot. Do not boil. Strain through sieve. Discard solids. Makes 3 1/2 cups (875 mL). Serves 4.

1 serving: 227 Calories; 0 g Total Fat (0 g Mono, 0 g Poly, 0 g Sat); 0 mg Cholesterol; 15 g Carbohydrate; 0 g Fibre; 0 g Protein; 15 mg Sodium

Cinnamon-Spiced Milkshake

If you've never had a spicy milkshake, this is the one to try!
Cinnamon and vanilla flavour a thick caramel shake.

Milk	2/3 cup	150 mL
Brown sugar, packed	1/4 cup	60 mL
Large marshmallows, quartered	6	6
Ground cinnamon	1/2 tsp.	2 mL
Vanilla ice cream	3 cups	750 mL
Milk	1 cup	250 mL

Measure first 4 ingredients into small saucepan. Heat and stir on medium until marshmallow is melted. Cool. Transfer to blender.

Add ice cream and second amount of milk. Process until smooth. Makes 5 1/2 cups (1.4 L). Serves 4.

1 serving: 251 Calories; 9.2 g Total Fat (2.7 g Mono, 0.3 g Poly, 5.7 g Sat); 37 mg Cholesterol; 39 g Carbohydrate; trace Fibre; 5 g Protein; 108 mg Sodium

Ginger Iced Tea

A favourite of those who enjoy ginger. Beautiful amber colour.

Coarsely grated, peeled gingerroot (not ground)	1/4 cup	60 mL
Water	5 cups	1.25 L
Granulated sugar	1 cup	250 mL
Whole loose orange pekoe (or your favourite) tea (about 6 tea bags)	1/4 cup	60 mL
Water	5 cups	1.25 L
Crushed ice (optional)		

Combine ginger and first amount of water in large bowl. Cover. Let stand for 24 hours.

(continued on next page)

Pour ginger mixture into medium saucepan. Add sugar. Heat and stir on medium for about 5 minutes until sugar is dissolved. Bring to a boil. Reduce heat to medium-low. Cover. Simmer for 10 minutes. Remove from heat. Strain through sieve into large bowl. Discard solids.

Add tea. Stir. Let stand for 10 minutes. Strain through sieve into large pitcher. Discard solids.

Add second amount of water. Stir. Cover. Chill for at least 4 hours until cold.

Serve over crushed ice. Makes 10 cups (2.5 L).

1 cup (250 mL): 83 Calories; 0 g Total Fat (0 g Mono, 0 g Poly, 0 g Sat); 0 mg Cholesterol; 21 g Carbohydrate; 0 g Fibre; 0 g Protein; 4 mg Sodium

Fresh Herb Tea

Reward yourself after the yard work is done with this soothing tea using herbs right from the garden. Chill any leftover tea to serve over ice the next day.

Fresh mint leaves	1/4 cup	60 mL
Fresh basil	2 tbsp.	30 mL
Fresh sage leaves	2	2
Fresh thyme leaves (about 5 inch, 12.5 cm, length)	2	2
Lemon grass, bulb only (root and stalk removed)	1	1
Piece of peeled gingerroot (1 inch, 2.5 cm, length), sliced thinly	1	1
Finely grated lemon zest	1 1/2 tsp.	7 mL
Boiling water	6 cups	1.5 L
Liquid honey (optional)	1 – 2 tsp.	5 – 10 mL

Rinse large teapot with hot water to warm. Add first 7 ingredients.

Pour boiling water over herb mixture. Cover. Let stand for 10 minutes. Strain through sieve. Discard solids.

Add honey. Stir. Makes 6 cups (1.5 L).

1 cup (250 mL): 0 Calories; 0 g Total Fat (0 g Mono, 0 g Poly, 0 g Sat); 0 mg Cholesterol; 0 g Carbohydrate; trace Fibre; 0 g Protein; 0 mg Sodium

Pictured on page 71 and on back cover.

Spicy Naan Bread

Crunchy, savoury flatbread. Serve with your favourite curry.

Warm water	2/3 cup	150 mL
Granulated sugar	1 tsp.	5 mL
Active dry yeast	1 tsp.	5 mL
All-purpose flour	2 cups	500 mL
Ground cumin	1 tsp.	5 mL
Ground coriander	1 tsp.	5 mL
Salt	1 tsp.	5 mL
Cayenne pepper	1/2 tsp.	2 mL
Hard margarine (or butter), melted	1/4 cup	60 mL
Plain yogurt	3 tbsp.	50 mL
All-purpose flour, approximately	3 tbsp.	50 mL
Hard margarine (or butter), melted	2 tbsp.	30 mL
Sesame seeds, toasted (see Tip, page 33)	1 tbsp.	15 mL

Stir water and sugar in small bowl until sugar is dissolved. Sprinkle yeast over top. Let stand for 10 minutes. Stir until yeast is dissolved.

Combine next 5 ingredients in large bowl. Make a well in centre.

Add first amount of margarine, yogurt and yeast mixture to well. Stir until soft dough forms. Turn out onto lightly floured surface. Knead for 5 to 10 minutes, adding second amount of flour 1 tbsp. (15 mL) at a time if necessary to prevent sticking, until smooth and elastic. Place in greased large bowl, turning once to grease top. Cover with greased waxed paper and tea towel. Let stand in oven with light on and door closed for about 1 1/2 hours until doubled in bulk. Punch dough down. Knead until smooth. Divide dough into 6 portions. Roll out each portion on lightly floured surface to 8 inch (20 cm) round. Cover rounds with damp tea towels to prevent drying. Place 1 round on greased baking sheet. Broil on top rack in oven for 1 1/2 to 2 minutes until puffed and starting to brown. Turn over. Broil for 1 to 2 minutes until starting to brown. Remove from oven.

Brush top with about 1/2 tsp. (2 mL) of second amount of margarine. Sprinkle with sesame seeds. Broil for 30 seconds until golden brown. Wrap baked bread in tea towel to keep warm. Repeat with remaining portions. Makes 6 naan breads.

1 naan bread: 303 Calories; 13.5 g Total Fat (8.2 g Mono, 1.7 g Poly, 2.7 g Sat); 0 mg Cholesterol; 39 g Carbohydrate; 2 g Fibre; 6 g Protein; 544 mg Sodium

Pictured on page 143.

Feta Herb Bread

Melt-in-your-mouth delicious! Try making this on the barbecue.

Cooking oil	1 tsp.	5 mL
Garlic cloves, minced	2	2
Hard margarine (or butter), softened	1/2 cup	125 mL
Crumbled feta cheese (about 2 1/2 oz., 70 g)	1/2 cup	125 mL
Sweet (or regular) chili sauce	2 tbsp.	30 mL
Chopped fresh basil (or 1 1/2 tsp., 7 mL, dried)	2 tbsp.	30 mL
Chopped fresh oregano leaves (or 1/2 tsp., 2 mL, dried)	2 tsp.	10 mL
French bread loaf, cut into 1/2 inch (12 mm) slices	1	1

Heat cooking oil in small frying pan on medium-low. Add garlic. Cook for 2 to 3 minutes, stirring often, until softened and fragrant but not browned. Transfer to small bowl. Cool.

Add next 5 ingredients. Stir well.

Spread margarine mixture on both sides of each bread slice. Arrange slices into loaf shape. Wrap in foil. Bake in 375°F (190°C) oven for about 25 minutes until heated through and crust is crisp. Makes 26 slices.

1 slice: 93 Calories; 5.1 g Total Fat (2.9 g Mono, 0.6 g Poly, 1.4 g Sat); 3 mg Cholesterol; 10 g Carbohydrate; 1 g Fibre; 2 g Protein; 203 mg Sodium

Pictured on page 71 and on back cover.

Paré Pointer

He asked when his salary increase would become effective and was told, "as soon as you do."

Spiced Fruit Scones

Tastes like Christmas! Serve warm,
spread with Peach Conserve, page 128.

Orange juice	1 cup	250 mL
Golden raisins	1/2 cup	125 mL
Diced mixed peel	1/4 cup	60 mL
All-purpose flour	3 cups	750 mL
Granulated sugar	1/4 cup	60 mL
Baking powder	2 tbsp.	30 mL
Ground cinnamon	1 tsp.	5 mL
Ground ginger	1 tsp.	5 mL
Ground cloves	1/4 tsp.	1 mL
Salt	1/4 tsp.	1 mL
Hard margarine (or butter), cut up	1/4 cup	60 mL

Combine orange juice, raisins and peel in small bowl. Let stand for 1 hour.

Measure next 7 ingredients into large bowl. Stir. Cut in margarine until mixture resembles coarse crumbs. Make a well in centre. Add orange juice mixture to well. Stir until just moistened. Turn out onto lightly floured surface. Knead 6 times. Divide in half. Roll out or press each half into 6 inch (15 cm) round, 1 inch (2.5 cm) thick. Place rounds 1 inch (2.5 cm) apart on greased baking sheet. Score top of each into 6 wedges with knife. Bake on centre rack in 450°F (230°C) oven for about 15 minutes until golden. Let stand on baking sheet for 5 minutes before serving. Each round cuts into 6 wedges, for a total of 12.

1 wedge: 217 Calories; 4.5 g Total Fat (2.7 g Mono, 0.6 g Poly, 0.9 g Sat); 0 mg Cholesterol; 41 g Carbohydrate; 2 g Fibre; 4 g Protein; 284 mg Sodium

Pictured on page 53.

Paré Pointer

He's like a blister. He shows up when the work is done.

Sun-Dried Tomato Muffins

Flavourful, savoury muffins best served warm from the oven.

All-purpose flour	2 1/2 cups	625 mL
Baking powder	1 1/2 tbsp.	25 mL
Crumbled feta cheese (about 4 oz., 113 g)	3/4 cup	175 mL
Grated Parmesan cheese	1/2 cup	125 mL
Chopped fresh parsley (or 2 1/4 tsp., 11 mL, flakes)	3 tbsp.	50 mL
Chopped fresh chives (or 2 1/4 tsp., 11 mL, dried)	3 tbsp.	50 mL
Chopped fresh rosemary leaves (or 1/4 tsp., 1 mL, dried)	1 tsp.	5 mL
Pepper	1/2 tsp.	2 mL
Large egg	1	1
Buttermilk (or reconstituted from powder)	1 cup	250 mL
Hard margarine (or butter), melted	1/3 cup	75 mL
Sun-dried tomatoes in oil, drained and chopped	1/3 cup	75 mL

Combine flour and baking powder in large bowl.

Add next 6 ingredients. Stir. Make a well in centre.

Beat remaining 4 ingredients with fork in small bowl. Add to well. Stir until just moistened. Batter will be stiff. Grease 12 muffin cups with cooking spray. Fill cups until full. Bake in 375°F (190°C) oven for about 25 minutes until tops are golden and wooden pick inserted in centre of muffin comes out clean. Let stand in pan for 5 minutes before serving. Makes 12 muffins.

1 muffin: 219 Calories; 10.2 g Total Fat (4.9 g Mono, 0.9 g Poly, 3.8 g Sat); 31 mg Cholesterol; 24 g Carbohydrate; 1 g Fibre; 8 g Protein; 436 mg Sodium

Pictured on page 72.

Fresh Herb Cheese Rolls

Flecks of herbs and cheese in tender, golden brown rolls. Serve with chili or stew.

All-purpose flour	2 cups	500 mL
Envelope of instant yeast (or 2 1/4 tsp., 11 mL)	1/4 oz.	8 g
Chopped fresh chives (or 1 1/2 tsp., 7 mL, dried)	2 tbsp.	30 mL
Chopped fresh parsley (or 3/4 tsp., 4 mL, flakes)	1 tbsp.	15 mL
Finely chopped fresh rosemary leaves (or 1/2 tsp., 2 mL, dried crushed)	2 tsp.	10 mL
Finely chopped fresh marjoram leaves (or 1/2 tsp., 2 mL, dried)	2 tsp.	10 mL
Seasoned Salt, page 14	3/4 tsp.	4 mL
Pepper	1/2 tsp.	2 mL
Onion powder	1/4 tsp.	1 mL
Milk	1 1/4 cups	300 mL
Hard margarine (or butter)	1/4 cup	60 mL
Granulated sugar	2 tbsp.	30 mL
Salt	1 tsp.	5 mL
Large egg, fork-beaten	1	1
Grated sharp Cheddar cheese	3/4 cup	175 mL
All-purpose flour, approximately	1 1/2 cups	375 mL
Hard margarine (or butter), melted (optional)	2 tsp.	10 mL

Measure first 9 ingredients into large bowl. Stir. Make a well in centre.

Heat and stir next 4 ingredients in small saucepan on medium until sugar is dissolved and margarine is almost melted. Remove from heat. Stir until margarine is melted. Let stand for 5 minutes. Pour into well. Add egg and cheese to well. Stir.

Slowly work in enough of second amount of flour until dough pulls away from side of bowl and is no longer sticky. Turn out onto lightly floured surface. Knead for 8 to 10 minutes, adding flour 1 tbsp. (15 mL) at a time if necessary while kneading to prevent sticking, until smooth and elastic. Place in separate greased large bowl, turning once to grease top. Cover with greased waxed paper and tea towel. Let stand in oven with light on and door closed for about 1 1/2 hours until doubled in bulk. Punch dough down. Knead until smooth.

(continued on next page)

Breads & Biscuits

Divide dough in half. Divide each half into 8 portions. Shape into balls. Arrange about 1 inch (2.5 cm) apart on greased baking sheet. Cover with greased waxed paper and tea towel. Let stand in oven with light on and door closed for about 45 minutes until almost doubled in size. Bake in 375°F (190°C) oven for about 20 minutes until golden brown and hollow sounding when tapped. Let stand on baking sheet for 5 minutes before removing to wire rack.

Brush tops of hot rolls with melted margarine. Cool Makes 16 rolls.

1 roll: 176 Calories; 5.8 g Total Fat (2.7 g Mono, 0.5 g Poly, 2.1 g Sat); 20 mg Cholesterol; 25 g Carbohydrate; 1 g Fibre; 6 g Protein; 242 mg Sodium

Pictured on front cover.

Corn Roti

Tasty, irregular-shaped flatbread, grilled to perfection. Serve with Yogurt Cucumber Side, page 123, or West Indian Relish, page 135.

Can of kernel corn, drained	12 oz.	341 mL
Cumin seed	2 tsp.	10 mL
Coarsely chopped fresh cilantro or parsley (or 1 1/2 tsp., 7 mL, dried)	2 tbsp.	30 mL
Cooking oil	1 tbsp.	15 mL
All-purpose flour	1 1/2 cups	375 mL
Salt	1 tsp.	5 mL
All-purpose flour, approximately	2 tbsp.	30 mL

Process first 4 ingredients in blender or food processor until smooth. Transfer to large bowl.

Add first amount of flour and salt. Mix until soft dough forms. Turn out onto lightly floured surface. Knead for 5 to 10 minutes, adding second amount of flour 1 tbsp. (15 mL) at a time if necessary to prevent sticking, until smooth and elastic. Wrap with plastic wrap. Let stand for 30 minutes. Divide dough into 12 portions. Roll out each portion on lightly floured surface into 5 inch (12.5 cm) round. Cover rounds with damp tea towel to prevent drying. Preheat electric grill for 5 minutes or gas barbecue to medium-high. Cook rounds on greased grill for 2 to 3 minutes per side until starting to crisp and grill marks appear. Makes 12 roti.

1 roti: 94 Calories; 1.5 g Total Fat (0.7 g Mono, 0.5 g Poly, 0.1 g Sat); 0 mg Cholesterol; 18 g Carbohydrate; 1 g Fibre; 2 g Protein; 259 mg Sodium

Pictured on page 53.

Salmon Dill Biscuits

Serve with a garden fresh salad for a light lunch.

All-purpose flour	2 cups	500 mL
Chopped fresh dill (or 2 1/4 tsp., 11 mL, dill weed)	3 tbsp.	50 mL
Baking powder	1 1/2 tbsp.	25 mL
Lemon pepper	1/2 tsp.	2 mL
Salt	1/4 tsp.	1 mL
Hard margarine (or butter)	1/4 cup	60 mL
Can of red salmon, drained, skin and round bones removed, flaked	7 1/2 oz.	213 g
Buttermilk (or reconstituted from powder)	1/2 cup	125 mL
Sour cream	1/4 cup	60 mL

Combine first 5 ingredients in large bowl. Cut in margarine until mixture resembles coarse crumbs. Make a well in centre.

Add salmon, buttermilk, and sour cream to well. Stir until just moistened. Turn out onto lightly floured surface. Knead 6 times. Roll out or press to 3/4 inch (2 cm) thickness. Cut out rounds with 2 inch (5 cm) biscuit cutter. Arrange, just touching, in greased 9 x 9 inch (22 x 22 cm) pan. Bake on centre rack in 450°F (230°C) oven for about 20 minutes until golden. Let stand in pan for 5 minutes before removing to wire rack to cool. Makes 16 biscuits.

1 biscuit: 115 Calories; 4.5 g Total Fat (2.4 g Mono, 0.6 g Poly, 1.2 g Sat); 7 mg Cholesterol; 14 g Carbohydrate; 1 g Fibre; 5 g Protein; 248 mg Sodium

Cheese Herb Scones

Serve warm scones (skahnz) with soup or stew for a warming winter meal.

All-purpose flour	2 cups	500 mL
Baking powder	2 tsp.	10 mL
Salt	1/2 tsp.	2 mL
Baking soda	1/2 tsp.	2 mL
Dried basil	1/2 tsp.	2 mL
Dried whole oregano	1/4 tsp.	1 mL
Dried thyme, just a pinch		
Hard margarine (or butter), cut up	1/4 cup	60 mL

(continued on next page)

Grated sharp Cheddar cheese	1 cup	250 mL
Milk	3/4 cup	175 mL
Liquid honey	1/4 cup	60 mL
Large eggs	2	2

Combine first 7 ingredients in large bowl. Cut in margarine until mixture resembles coarse crumbs. Make a well in centre.

Combine next 4 ingredients in small bowl. Add to well. Stir until just moistened. Spoon into greased 8 inch (20 cm) round pan. Spread evenly. Bake in 350°F (175°C) oven for 30 to 35 minutes until wooden pick inserted in centre comes out clean. Let stand in pan on wire rack until cool. Cuts into 12 wedges.

1 wedge: 203 Calories; 8.6 g Total Fat (4 g Mono, 0.7 g Poly, 3.3 g Sat); 47 mg Cholesterol; 25 g Carbohydrate; 1 g Fibre; 6 g Protein; 343 mg Sodium

Pictured on page 53.

Herb Bread

A great addition to your favourite pasta dinner. Quick and easy to prepare.

Hard margarine (or butter), softened	1/2 cup	125 mL
Parsley flakes	2 1/4 tsp.	11 mL
Dried basil	1 tsp.	5 mL
Ground marjoram	1 tsp.	5 mL
Lemon juice	1 tsp.	5 mL
Garlic powder	1/4 tsp.	1 mL
Dried thyme	1/8 tsp.	0.5 mL
French bread loaf, cut into 1 inch (2.5 cm) slices	1	1

Combine first 7 ingredients in small bowl.

Spread margarine mixture on both sides of each bread slice. Arrange slices into loaf shape. Wrap in foil. Bake in 375°F (190°C) oven for about 25 minutes until heated through and crust is crisp. Makes 14 slices.

1 slice: 151 Calories; 7.9 g Total Fat (4.9 g Mono, 0.9 g Poly, 1.6 g Sat); 0 mg Cholesterol; 17 g Carbohydrate; 1 g Fibre; 3 g Protein; 279 mg Sodium

Pictured on page 125.

Mushroom Broccoli Salad

A chunky salad with an inviting mix of fresh ingredients.
The tangy dill dressing is irresistible!

Broccoli florets	4 cups	1 L
Water		
Ice water		
Sliced fresh white mushrooms	2 cups	500 mL
Fresh pea pods, trimmed	2 cups	500 mL
Slivered almonds, toasted (see Tip, page 33)	1/2 cup	125 mL
MUSTARD DILL DRESSING		
Buttermilk (or reconstituted from powder)	1/4 cup	60 mL
Peanut (or cooking) oil	3 tbsp.	50 mL
Red wine vinegar	2 tbsp.	30 mL
Dijon mustard (with whole seeds)	1 tbsp.	15 mL
Chopped fresh dill (or 3/4 tsp., 4 mL, dill weed)	1 tbsp.	15 mL
Garlic clove, minced (or 1/4 tsp., 1 mL, powder)	1	1
Salt	1/4 tsp.	1 mL
Pepper	1/4 tsp.	1 mL

Cook broccoli in water in large saucepan until tender-crisp. Immediately plunge into large bowl of ice water. Let stand for 10 minutes. Drain well. Return broccoli to bowl.

Add mushrooms, pea pods and almonds. Toss.

Mustard Dill Dressing: Measure all 8 ingredients into jar with tight-fitting lid. Shake well. Makes 2/3 cup (150 mL) dressing. Drizzle over broccoli mixture. Toss until coated. Makes about 8 1/2 cups (2.1 L).

1 cup (250 mL): 128 Calories; 9.5 g Total Fat (5 g Mono, 2.7 g Poly, 1.3 g Sat); 0 mg Cholesterol; 8 g Carbohydrate; 2 g Fibre; 5 g Protein; 117 mg Sodium

Pictured on page 89.

Tomato And Feta Salad

Fresh and flavourful. Sesame Walnut Topping is a great addition to this or any salad.

SESAME WALNUT TOPPING

Finely chopped walnuts	2 tbsp.	30 mL
Sesame seeds	1 tbsp.	15 mL
Cumin seed	1/2 tsp.	2 mL
Large tomatoes, quartered, seeds removed, chopped (about 2 2/3 cups, 650 mL)	4	4
Crumbled feta cheese (about 4 oz., 113 g)	3/4 cup	175 mL
Thinly sliced red onion	1/2 cup	125 mL
Pitted kalamata (Greek) olives	1/4 cup	60 mL
Chopped fresh mint leaves	3 tbsp.	50 mL
Chopped fresh parsley	2 tbsp.	30 mL
Olive (or cooking) oil	2 tbsp.	30 mL
Lemon juice	2 tbsp.	30 mL
Pepper	1/4 tsp.	1 mL

Sesame Walnut Topping: Heat and stir first 3 ingredients in small frying pan on medium for about 3 minutes until fragrant. Transfer to small cup. Set aside to cool. Makes about 1/4 cup (60 mL) topping.

Measure next 6 ingredients into large bowl. Toss.

Add olive oil, lemon juice and pepper. Toss. Divide among 4 salad plates. Divide and sprinkle topping over each. Serves 4.

1 serving: 224 Calories; 17.5 g Total Fat (7.8 g Mono, 3 g Poly, 5.7 g Sat); 26 mg Cholesterol; 12 g Carbohydrate; 3 g Fibre; 7 g Protein; 381 mg Sodium

Pictured on page 54.

Paré Pointer
We have two chances of being very wealthy—slim and none.

Date And Orange Salad

Serve this on a bed of crisp lettuce or add your favourite greens and toss them together. A pleasing combination either way.

Water	2/3 cup	150 mL
Liquid honey	3 tbsp.	50 mL
Star anise	1	1
Cinnamon stick (4 inches, 10 cm)	1	1
Pitted dates, halved lengthwise	3/4 cup	175 mL
Medium oranges, peeled and segmented	6	6
Thinly sliced dried apricots	1/3 cup	75 mL
Whole blanched almonds, toasted (see Tip, page 33)	1/4 cup	60 mL

Measure first 4 ingredients into small frying pan. Stir. Bring to a boil on medium-high. Mixture will be foaming and bubbly. Boil for 5 to 10 minutes, stirring occasionally, until reduced by about half. Remove from heat.

Add dates. Stir. Let stand for about 20 minutes until cool. Transfer to large bowl.

Add orange segments and apricot slices. Stir. Cover. Chill for at least 4 hours until cold. Remove and discard star anise and cinnamon stick.

Add almonds. Stir. Makes 2 3/4 cups (675 mL). Serves 4.

1 serving: 322 Calories; 5.5 g Total Fat (3.4 g Mono, 1.1 g Poly, 0.5 g Sat); 0 mg Cholesterol; 71 g Carbohydrate; 9 g Fibre; 5 g Protein; 4 mg Sodium

Pictured on page 54.

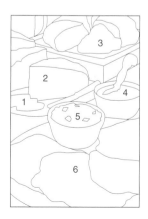

1. Tomato Basil Butter, page 127
2. Cheese Herb Scones, page 48
3. Spiced Fruit Scones, page 44
4. Spiced Peach Topping, page 128
5. West Indian Relish, page 135
6. Corn Roti, page 47

Props Courtesy Of: Corelle®
Island Pottery Inc.

Creamy Celery Seed Slaw

Serve with ribs or barbecued pork chops.
This will keep in the refrigerator for up to two days.

CELERY SEED DRESSING

Mayonnaise	1 cup	250 mL
Apple cider vinegar	2 tbsp.	30 mL
Granulated sugar	2 tbsp.	30 mL
Chopped fresh parsley (or 3/4 tsp., 4 mL, flakes)	1 tbsp.	15 mL
Celery seed	1 1/2 tsp.	7 mL
Salt	1/4 tsp.	1 mL
Shredded green cabbage, packed	3 cups	750 mL
Shredded red cabbage, packed	2 cups	500 mL
Grated carrot	3/4 cup	175 mL
Thinly sliced green onion	1/4 cup	60 mL

Celery Seed Dressing: Measure first 6 ingredients into large bowl. Stir until sugar is dissolved. Makes 1 1/4 cups (300 mL) dressing.

Add next 4 ingredients. Toss until coated. Cover. Chill for 1 hour to blend flavours. Makes 4 cups (1 L). Serves 6.

1 serving: 326 Calories; 31.5 g Total Fat (17.4 g Mono, 10.5 g Poly, 3 g Sat); 23 mg Cholesterol; 11 g Carbohydrate; 2 g Fibre; 2 g Protein; 316 mg Sodium

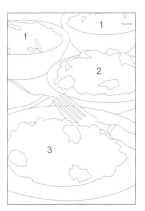

1. Satay Pork Salad, page 56
2. Date And Orange Salad, page 52
3. Tomato And Feta Salad, page 51

Props Courtesy Of: Casa Bugatti
                   Pfaltzgraff Canada

Satay Pork Salad

Colourful, crunchy salad with peanut-flavoured dressing.

Pork tenderloin, trimmed of fat	3/4 lb.	340 g
Salt, sprinkle		
SATAY DRESSING		
Warm water	1/3 cup	75 mL
Smooth peanut butter	1/3 cup	75 mL
Sweet chili sauce	1/4 cup	60 mL
Brown sugar, packed	2 tbsp.	30 mL
White wine vinegar	2 tbsp.	30 mL
Garlic cloves, minced (or 1/2 tsp., 2 mL, powder)	2	2
Fish sauce	1 tsp.	5 mL
Fresh bean sprouts (about 5 1/2 oz., 150 g)	2 cups	500 mL
Julienned English cucumber (with peel), see Note	1 cup	250 mL
Medium carrots, peeled lengthwise into 4 inch ribbons	2	2
Thinly sliced red onion	3/4 cup	175 mL
Unsalted peanuts, toasted (see Tip, page 33)	1/3 cup	75 mL
Chopped fresh cilantro (or parsley), packed	1/4 cup	60 mL
Shredded (long thread) coconut, toasted (see Tip, page 33)	1/4 cup	60 mL

Sprinkle pork with salt. Bake in 350°F (175°C) oven on greased wire rack set in baking sheet with sides for 35 to 40 minutes until meat thermometer inserted into thickest part of roast reads 155°F (68°C). Remove from oven. Cover with foil. Let stand for 10 minutes. Internal temperature should rise to at least 160°F (70°C). Cut into 1/4 inch (6 mm) thick slices. Transfer to extra-large bowl.

Satay Dressing: Measure first 7 ingredients into jar with tight-fitting lid. Shake well. Makes about 1 cup (250 mL) dressing. Add 1/2 of dressing to pork slices. Toss until coated.

Add next 6 ingredients. Toss. Transfer to serving bowl. Drizzle remaining dressing over top.

(continued on next page)

Salads

Sprinkle with coconut. Makes 4 1/2 cups (1.1 L). Serves 4.

1 serving: 456 Calories; 25.5 g Total Fat (10.5 g Mono, 5.7 g Poly, 7.8 g Sat); 54 mg Cholesterol; 32 g Carbohydrate; 6 g Fibre; 30 g Protein; 506 mg Sodium

Pictured on page 54.

Note: To cut vegetables julienne, cut into 1/8 inch (3 mm) strips that resemble matchsticks.

Springy Pasta Salad

Bouncy fusilli pasta and fresh flavours give this salad its name.

Olive (or cooking) oil	6 tbsp.	100 mL
Tarragon Garlic Vinegar, page 132 (see Note)	2 tbsp.	30 mL
Coarse ground pepper	1 tsp.	5 mL
Granulated sugar	1/2 tsp.	2 mL
Worcestershire sauce	1/4 tsp.	1 mL
Cooked fusilli pasta (about 5 oz., 140 g, uncooked), rinsed with cold water	2 cups	500 mL
Can of sliced ripe olives, drained	7 oz.	200 mL
Can of solid white tuna packed in water, drained	6 oz.	170 g
Crumbled feta cheese (about 2 1/2 oz., 70 g)	1/2 cup	125 mL
Diced red pepper	1/2 cup	125 mL
Grated Parmesan cheese	1/4 cup	60 mL
Chopped fresh parsley	1/4 cup	60 mL
Chopped fresh basil	2 tbsp.	30 mL

Process first 5 ingredients in blender until slightly thickened.

Measure next 8 ingredients into large bowl. Stir. Add olive oil mixture. Toss until pasta is coated. Makes 5 cups (1.25 L). Serves 4.

1 serving: 487 Calories; 31.6 g Total Fat (19.3 g Mono, 2.8 g Poly, 7.8 g Sat); 39 mg Cholesterol; 32 g Carbohydrate; 2 g Fibre; 20 g Protein; 746 mg Sodium

Note: Substitute 2 tbsp. (30 mL) white vinegar, 1/4 to 1/2 tsp. (1 to 2 mL) dried tarragon and 1/8 tsp. (0.5 mL) garlic powder for the Tarragon Garlic Vinegar.

Cranberry Salad

An elegant starter salad bursting with sweet, tangy flavour.
A perfect accompaniment to roast chicken or turkey.

CRANBERRY DRESSING

Olive (or cooking) oil	3 tbsp.	50 mL
Frozen concentrated cranberry juice, thawed	2 tbsp.	30 mL
Golden corn syrup	2 tbsp.	30 mL
Red wine vinegar	2 tbsp.	30 mL
Garlic clove, minced (or 1/4 tsp., 1 mL, powder)	1	1
Cayenne pepper	1/4 tsp.	1 mL
Salt	1/4 tsp.	1 mL
Pepper, sprinkle		
Dried cranberries	2/3 cup	150 mL
Mixed salad greens	6 cups	1.5 L
Shaved Parmesan cheese	1/2 cup	125 mL
Chopped pecans, toasted (see Tip, page 33)	1/4 cup	60 mL
Finely chopped fresh basil	3 tbsp.	50 mL

Cranberry Dressing: Measure first 8 ingredients into jar with tight-fitting lid. Shake well. Makes 1/2 cup (125 mL) dressing. Pour into medium bowl.

Add cranberries. Stir until coated. Cover. Let stand for 3 hours to blend flavours. Strain through sieve, reserving cranberries and dressing in separate small bowls.

Arrange 1 cup (250 mL) salad greens on each of 6 salad plates. Divide and scatter cranberries, Parmesan cheese, pecans and fresh basil over salad greens. Divide and drizzle dressing over each. Serves 6.

1 serving: 208 Calories; 13.5 g Total Fat (8 g Mono, 1.5 g Poly, 2.9 g Sat); 7 mg Cholesterol; 19 g Carbohydrate; 3 g Fibre; 6 g Protein; 295 mg Sodium

Pictured on page 107.

Paré Pointer

At times the least little thing will set a person off,
although some are self-starters.

Salads

Potato Mint Salad

Fresh mint and cashews add an unexpected flair to potato salad.
Light, slightly sweet dressing will have them asking for more.

Medium red potatoes (with skin), about 3 lbs. (1.4 kg)	6	6
Water		
Salt, just a pinch		
CREAMY MINT DRESSING		
Sour cream	1/2 cup	125 mL
Coarsely chopped fresh mint leaves	1/4 cup	60 mL
Liquid honey	2 tbsp.	30 mL
Lemon juice	2 tbsp.	30 mL
Dry mustard	2 tsp.	10 mL
Salt	1/2 tsp.	2 mL
Pepper	1/2 tsp.	2 mL
Finely chopped red pepper	1/2 cup	125 mL
Unsalted cashews, toasted (see Tip, page 33), optional	3 tbsp.	50 mL
Chopped fresh chives, for garnish	2 tbsp.	30 mL

Cook whole potatoes in water and salt in large pot or Dutch oven for about 40 minutes until just tender. Drain. Let stand until cool enough to handle. Cut each potato in half lengthwise. Cut each half crosswise into 1/2 inch (12 mm) slices. Transfer to large bowl.

Creamy Mint Dressing: Process first 7 ingredients in blender or food processor until smooth. Makes 3/4 cup (175 mL) dressing.

Add red pepper and cashews to potato slices. Toss. Drizzle with dressing. Toss until coated.

Sprinkle with chives. Makes 8 cups (2 L). Serves 6.

1 serving: 174 Calories; 3.4 g Total Fat (1.1 g Mono, 0.3 g Poly, 1.8 g Sat); 8 mg Cholesterol; 33 g Carbohydrate; 3 g Fibre; 4 g Protein; 218 mg Sodium

Pictured on page 89.

Oriental Pork Salad

Colourful greens, crunchy vegetables and noodles
dress up pork for lunch or dinner.

Chopped fresh cilantro or parsley (or 2 1/4 tsp., 11 mL, dried)	3 tbsp.	50 mL
Liquid honey	2 tbsp.	30 mL
Soy sauce	2 tbsp.	30 mL
Garlic cloves, minced (or 1/2 tsp., 2 mL, powder)	2	2
Finely grated, peeled gingerroot	1 tsp.	5 mL
Chinese five-spice powder	1/2 tsp.	2 mL
Pork tenderloin, trimmed of fat, cut into 1/4 inch (6 mm) thick slices	3/4 lb.	340 g
Cooking oil	1 tbsp.	15 mL
Mixed salad greens	4 cups	1 L
Sliced English cucumber (with peel)	1 cup	250 mL
Thinly sliced green onion	1 cup	250 mL
Sliced radish	1 cup	250 mL
Can of sliced water chestnuts, drained	8 oz.	227 mL
ORIENTAL DRESSING		
Cooking oil	1/4 cup	60 mL
White vinegar	2 tbsp.	30 mL
Granulated sugar	1/2 tsp.	2 mL
Coarse ground pepper	1/2 tsp.	2 mL
Chinese five-spice powder	1/8 tsp.	0.5 mL
Salt, just a pinch		
Bag of chow mein noodles	4 oz.	113 g

Measure first 6 ingredients into medium bowl. Stir. Add pork. Stir until coated.

Heat wok or large frying pan on medium-high until very hot. Add cooking oil. Add pork mixture. Stir-fry for 3 to 5 minutes until pork is no longer pink and liquid is evaporated. Remove from heat.

Combine next 5 ingredients in large salad bowl.

(continued on next page)

Oriental Dressing: Measure first 6 ingredients into jar with tight-fitting lid. Shake well. Makes about 1/3 cup (75 mL) dressing. Drizzle over salad greens. Add pork mixture. Toss.

Scatter noodles over top. Serve immediately. Makes 9 1/2 cups (2.4 L).

1 cup (250 mL): 221 Calories; 13.3 g Total Fat (6.2 g Mono, 4.6 g Poly, 1.7 g Sat); 20 mg Cholesterol; 16 g Carbohydrate; 2 g Fibre; 10 g Protein; 301 mg Sodium

Pictured on page 90.

Seashell Pasta Salad

Pretty green herbs and pink shrimp tossed with shell pasta.

Large shell pasta (about 5 oz., 140 g)	2 cups	500 mL
Boiling water		
Salt		
Chopped green onion	1/2 cup	125 mL
Grated Parmesan cheese	1/3 cup	75 mL
Cooking oil	1/3 cup	75 mL
Tarragon Garlic Vinegar, page 132 (see Note)	1/3 cup	75 mL
Chopped fresh basil	2 tsp.	10 mL
Chopped fresh parsley	2 tsp.	10 mL
Chopped fresh oregano	1 tsp.	5 mL
Diced mozzarella (or havarti) cheese	1 cup	250 mL
Can of small shrimp, drained	3 1/2 oz.	100 g

Cook pasta in boiling water and salt in large uncovered pot or Dutch oven for 10 to 12 minutes, stirring occasionally, until tender but firm. Drain. Rinse with cold water. Drain. Transfer to large bowl.

Combine next 7 ingredients in small bowl. Add to pasta. Toss until coated.

Add mozzarella cheese and shrimp. Toss. Cover. Chill for about 4 hours until cold. Toss just before serving. Makes about 4 cups (1 L).

1 cup (250 mL): 477 Calories; 30.6 g Total Fat (14.6 g Mono, 6.4 g Poly, 8 g Sat); 74 mg Cholesterol; 30 g Carbohydrate; 1 g Fibre; 21 g Protein; 342 mg Sodium

Pictured on page 71.

Note: Substitute 2 tbsp. (30 mL) white vinegar, 1/4 to 1/2 tsp. (1 to 2 mL) dried tarragon and 1/8 tsp. (0.5 mL) garlic powder for the Tarragon Garlic Vinegar.

Mulligatawny Soup

Creamy, curry-coloured soup with flecks of green cilantro.
Wonderfully satisfying flavour, texture and aroma!

Cooking oil	2 tsp.	10 mL
Chopped onion	1 1/2 cups	375 mL
Whole green cardamom pods, bruised (see Tip, page 83)	6	6
Garlic cloves, minced (or 3/4 tsp., 4 mL, powder)	3	3
Cinnamon stick (4 inches, 10 cm)	1	1
Finely grated, peeled gingerroot	2 tsp.	10 mL
Ground cumin	1 tsp.	5 mL
Turmeric	1 tsp.	5 mL
Chili powder	1 tsp.	5 mL
Ground cloves	1/4 tsp.	1 mL
Peeled, diced potato	2 cups	500 mL
Diced carrot	1 cup	250 mL
Peeled, diced cooking apple (such as McIntosh)	1 cup	250 mL
Prepared chicken broth	4 cups	1 L
Lemon juice	2 tbsp.	30 mL
Can of coconut milk	14 oz.	398 mL
Finely chopped fresh cilantro or parsley (optional)	3 tbsp.	50 mL

Heat cooking oil in large pot or Dutch oven on medium. Add onion. Cook for 5 to 10 minutes, stirring often, until softened.

Add next 8 ingredients. Heat and stir for about 1 minute until fragrant.

Add next 5 ingredients. Stir. Bring to a boil. Reduce heat to medium-low. Cover. Simmer for 20 to 25 minutes, stirring occasionally, until vegetables are tender. Remove from heat. Let stand for 5 minutes. Remove and discard cardamom and cinnamon stick. Process vegetable mixture, in 2 batches, in blender or food processor until smooth. Return to same pot.

Add coconut milk and cilantro. Heat and stir on medium for about 10 minutes until hot. Makes 8 cups (2 L).

1 cup (250 mL): 192 Calories; 12.4 g Total Fat (1.4 g Mono, 0.7 g Poly, 9.4 g Sat); 0 mg Cholesterol; 17 g Carbohydrate; 2 g Fibre; 5 g Protein; 437 mg Sodium

Tomato And Fennel Soup

Beans add body and texture to this delicious soup. Chilies add spice.

Olive (or cooking) oil	2 tbsp.	30 mL
Chopped fennel bulbs (white part only), about 2	3 cups	750 mL
Chopped red onion	1 cup	250 mL
Garlic cloves, minced	4	4
Dried crushed chilies	1/2 – 1 tsp.	2 – 5 mL
Large tomatoes, peeled (see Tip, below) and chopped (about 2 1/2 cups, 625 mL)	4	4
Can of navy beans, drained and rinsed	14 oz.	398 mL
Prepared chicken (or vegetable) broth	6 cups	1.5 L
Tomato paste (see Tip, page 87)	1/4 cup	60 mL
Granulated sugar	1/4 tsp.	1 mL
Chopped fresh parsley	1/4 cup	60 mL

Heat olive oil in large pot or Dutch oven on medium. Add next 4 ingredients. Cook, uncovered, for 5 to 10 minutes, stirring often, until fennel is softened.

Add next 5 ingredients. Stir. Bring to a boil. Reduce heat to low. Cover. Simmer for about 30 minutes, stirring occasionally, until fennel is very soft.

Add parsley. Stir well. Makes about 12 cups (3 L).

1 cup (250 mL): 103 Calories; 3.5 g Total Fat (2 g Mono, 0.5 g Poly, 0.6 g Sat); 0 mg Cholesterol; 14 g Carbohydrate; 2 g Fibre; 6 g Protein; 486 mg Sodium

 To peel tomatoes, cut an X just through skin on bottom of tomatoes. Plunge into boiling water for 30 seconds, then immediately into bowl of ice cold water. Peel skin.

Spicy Yam Soup

A lovely, autumn soup with sweet yam and corn. Just a hint of heat.
Just as good using sweet potato.

Hard margarine (or butter)	2 tbsp.	30 mL
Thinly sliced onion	2 cups	500 mL
Garlic cloves, minced	4	4
Paprika	2 tsp.	10 mL
Ground coriander	1 tsp.	5 mL
Cayenne pepper	1/4 – 1/2 tsp.	1 – 2 mL
Yams, peeled and cut into 1 1/2 inch (3.8 cm) cubes (about 5 cups, 1.25 L)	2 lbs.	900 g
Prepared chicken broth	8 cups	2 L
Can of cream-style corn	14 oz.	398 mL
Pepper, sprinkle		
Sour cream, for garnish	1/4 cup	60 mL
Chopped fresh chives, for garnish	1/4 cup	60 mL

Melt margarine in large pot or Dutch oven on medium. Add onion. Cook, uncovered, for 5 to 10 minutes, stirring often, until softened.

Add next 4 ingredients. Heat and stir for 1 to 2 minutes until fragrant.

Add yam. Toss until coated.

Add broth. Stir. Bring to a boil. Reduce heat to medium-low. Cover. Simmer for 25 to 30 minutes, stirring occasionally, until yam is tender. Remove from heat. Let stand for 5 minutes. Process yam mixture, in 2 batches, in blender or food processor until smooth. Return to same pot.

Add corn and pepper. Stir. Bring to a boil on medium-high. Heat and stir for 3 to 4 minutes until heated through.

Ladle soup into 8 individual bowls. Swirl a dollop of sour cream through centre of each. Sprinkle chives over top. Makes 8 cups (2 L).

1 cup (250 mL): 243 Calories; 5 g Total Fat (2.6 g Mono, 0.8 g Poly, 1.1 g Sat); 0 mg Cholesterol; 43 g Carbohydrate; 6 g Fibre; 8 g Protein; 1018 mg Sodium

Pictured on page 71 and on back cover.

Chunky Zucchini Soup

A slow cooker recipe. Pleasant combination of dill, ham and zucchini.
Omit processing step if you like your soup extra-chunky.

Medium zucchini (with peel), quartered lengthwise and cut into 3/4 inch (2 cm) pieces (about 1 1/2 lbs., 680 g)	3	3
Potatoes, peeled and cut into 3/4 inch (2 cm) cubes (about 3 cups, 750 mL)	1 lb.	454 g
All-purpose flour	1/4 cup	60 mL
Prepared chicken broth	6 cups	1.5 L
Leeks (white and tender green parts), sliced thinly (about 3 cups, 750 mL)	3	3
Chopped fresh dill (or 2 1/4 tsp., 11 mL, dill weed)	3 tbsp.	50 mL
Chopped cooked ham	1 1/2 cups	375 mL
Evaporated milk (or half-and-half cream)	1 cup	250 mL
Chopped fresh dill (or 1 1/4 tsp., 6 mL, dill weed)	1 1/2 tbsp.	25 mL
Salt, sprinkle		
Pepper, sprinkle		

Put zucchini, potato and flour into 4 to 5 quart (4 to 5 L) slow cooker. Stir until coated.

Add broth, leek and first amount of dill. Stir. Cover. Cook on Low for 8 to 9 hours, or on High for 4 to 4 1/2 hours, until vegetables are tender. Carefully transfer 3 to 4 cups (750 mL to 1 L) of vegetables from broth to blender or food processor using slotted spoon. Process until smooth. Return to slow cooker.

Add ham, evaporated milk and second amount of dill. Stir. Cover. Cook on High for about 10 minutes until heated through.

Add salt and pepper. Stir well. Makes 12 cups (3 L).

1 cup (250 mL): 152 Calories; 4.4 g Total Fat (1.7 g Mono, 0.6 g Poly, 1.9 g Sat); 17 mg Cholesterol; 18 g Carbohydrate; 2 g Fibre; 11 g Protein; 721 mg Sodium

Curried Chicken Soup

Golden, fragrant soup with lots of chicken.

Whole chicken, skin removed, cut into serving-size portions (or bone-in chicken parts, skin removed)	3 lbs.	1.4 kg
Diced carrot	1 cup	250 mL
Chopped onion	1 cup	250 mL
Diced celery rib	1/2 cup	125 mL
Chicken bouillon powder	2 tbsp.	30 mL
Whole cloves	2	2
Pepper	1/4 tsp.	1 mL
Water	6 cups	1.5 L
Hard margarine (or butter)	1/3 cup	75 mL
Chopped onion	1 cup	250 mL
Peeled, sliced cooking apple (such as McIntosh)	3/4 cup	175 mL
Curry powder	1 tbsp.	15 mL
Turmeric	1/2 tsp.	2 mL
All-purpose flour	1/3 cup	75 mL
Cayenne pepper	1/2 tsp.	2 mL
Hot cooked rice (optional)	2 cups	500 mL
Lemon slices	8	8

Place chicken in large pot or Dutch oven. Add next 7 ingredients. Stir. Bring to a boil on medium-high. Reduce heat to medium-low. Cover. Simmer for about 40 minutes, stirring occasionally, until chicken is tender. Remove and discard cloves. Remove chicken to large plate using slotted spoon. Let stand until cool enough to handle. Remove meat from bones. Discard bones. Chop meat coarsely. Return to vegetable mixture.

Melt margarine in large frying pan on medium. Add next 4 ingredients. Heat and stir for 5 to 10 minutes until onion and apple are softened.

Add flour and cayenne pepper. Heat and stir for 2 minutes. Slowly add 2 cups (500 mL) broth from chicken mixture, stirring constantly, until boiling and thickened. Add to chicken mixture. Stir until combined and heated through. Makes about 10 cups (2.5 L).

(continued on next page)

Place about 1/4 cup (60 mL) rice and 1 lemon slice in each of 8 bowls. Divide and ladle soup over top. Serves 8.

1 serving: 232 Calories; 11.2 g Total Fat (6.1 g Mono, 1.6 g Poly, 2.4 g Sat); 58 mg Cholesterol; 13 g Carbohydrate; 2 g Fibre; 20 g Protein; 667 mg Sodium

Pictured on page 72.

Vegetable Soup

Bouquet garni adds lots of flavour to this simple but delicious soup.

Diced onion	3/4 cup	175 mL
Diced carrot	3/4 cup	175 mL
Peeled, diced potato	3/4 cup	175 mL
Diced yellow turnip	1/4 cup	60 mL
Diced celery rib, with leaves	1/4 cup	60 mL
Water	2 1/2 cups	625 mL
Granulated sugar	1/4 tsp.	1 mL
Salt	1 tsp.	5 mL
Pepper	1/8 tsp.	0.5 mL
Bouquet garni (see Note)	1	1
Tomato juice	1 cup	250 mL
Vegetable bouillon powder	1 tsp.	5 mL
Chopped fresh thyme leaves (optional)	1/2 tsp.	2 mL
Chopped fresh parsley (optional)	1/2 tsp.	2 mL

Combine first 9 ingredients in large pot or Dutch oven. Tie bouquet garni to pot handle. Submerge in liquid. Bring to a boil on medium-high. Reduce heat to medium. Cover. Simmer for about 25 minutes, stirring occasionally, until vegetables are tender. Remove and discard bouquet garni.

Add tomato juice and bouillon powder. Stir. Bring to a boil, stirring occasionally, until heated through. Divide between 2 soup bowls.

Divide and sprinkle thyme and parsley over top of each. Makes about 3 1/2 cups (875 mL).

1 cup (250 mL): 77 Calories; 0.4 g Total Fat (0.1 g Mono, 0.1 g Poly, 0.1 g Sat); 0 mg Cholesterol; 18 g Carbohydrate; 3 g Fibre; 2 g Protein; 1171 mg Sodium

Pictured on page 72.

Note: A classic bouquet garni combines 4 sprigs of fresh parsley, 3 sprigs of fresh thyme and 1 bay leaf. Lay herbs in 10 inch (25 cm) square cheesecloth. Draw up corners and tie with butcher's string.

Indonesian Chicken Soup

A most attractive and flavourful dish. Filling and hearty.

CHICKEN STOCK		
Bone-in chicken breast halves (backs attached), skin removed	2	2
Chopped onion	1 cup	250 mL
Chopped celery rib, with leaves	3/4 cup	175 mL
Chopped carrot	1/2 cup	125 mL
Water	8 cups	2 L
SPICE PASTE		
Garlic cloves	5	5
Piece of peeled gingerroot (1/2 inch, 12 mm, length)	1	1
Chopped shallot (or green onion)	1	1
Dried crushed chilies	1/2 tsp.	2 mL
Turmeric	1/4 tsp.	1 mL
Cooking oil	1 tbsp.	15 mL
Shredded suey choy (Chinese cabbage)	1 1/2 cups	375 mL
Lemon grass, bulb only (root and stalk removed), bruised (see Tip, page 69)	1	1
Salt	1 1/2 tsp.	7 mL
Pepper	1/8 tsp.	0.5 mL
Rice stick noodles, broken up (about 1/3 of 9 oz., 250 g, package)	3 1/2 oz.	100 g
Fresh bean sprouts (about 4 oz., 113 g), for garnish	1 1/2 cups	375 mL
Thinly sliced green onion, for garnish	6 tbsp.	100 mL

Chicken Stock: Place chicken breast halves in large pot or Dutch oven. Add next 4 ingredients. Bring to a boil on medium-high. Reduce heat to medium-low. Simmer for about 2 hours, stirring occasionally, until chicken is tender. Remove from heat. Remove chicken to large plate using slotted spoon. Let stand until cool enough to handle. Remove meat from bones. Discard bones. Shred meat with fork. Set aside. You should have about 2 1/4 cups (550 mL) chicken. Strain stock through sieve into large bowl. Discard solids. Makes about 5 1/2 cups (1.4 L) chicken stock. Set aside.

(continued on next page)

Spice Paste: Process first 5 ingredients in blender or food processor until smooth. Makes 1/4 cup (60 mL) paste.

Combine cooking oil and spice paste in same large pot or Dutch oven. Heat and stir on medium-low for 1 to 2 minutes until fragrant. Add chicken stock. Stir. Bring to a boil on medium-high, stirring occasionally.

Add chicken and next 4 ingredients. Stir. Add noodles. Stir well. Reduce heat to medium-low. Cover. Simmer for about 3 minutes, stirring several times, until cabbage is tender and noodles are tender but firm. Remove and discard lemon grass bulb.

Divide soup among 6 soup bowls. Top each with 1/4 cup (60 mL) bean sprouts. Scatter 1 tbsp. (15 mL) green onion over sprouts. Makes about 6 cups (1.5 L).

1 cup (250 mL): 149 Calories; 3.4 g Total Fat (1.6 g Mono, 0.9 g Poly, 0.4 g Sat); 27 mg Cholesterol; 17 g Carbohydrate; 1 g Fibre; 12 g Protein; 600 mg Sodium

Pictured on page 72.

 tip   *To bruise lemon grass bulb, hit bulb with mallet or flat side of wide knife to bruise or open slightly.*

Paré Pointer

His wife is losing two pounds a week.
He figures that in less than two years, he'll be rid of her.

Spiced Butter Chicken

Mildly spiced, tantalizing chicken.
Use herbs other than cilantro or parsley for a new flavour.

Butter (or hard margarine), softened	3 tbsp.	50 mL
Chopped fresh cilantro (or parsley)	2 tbsp.	30 mL
Finely grated orange peel	1 tsp.	5 mL
Ground cinnamon	1/2 tsp.	2 mL
Ground ginger	1/2 tsp.	2 mL
Chili powder	1/2 tsp.	2 mL
Salt	1/4 tsp.	1 mL
Pepper	1/4 tsp.	1 mL
Whole roasting chicken	4 lbs.	1.8 kg

Combine first 8 ingredients in small bowl.

Place chicken, backbone up, on cutting board. Cut down both sides of backbone, using kitchen shears or knife, to remove. Turn chicken over. Press chicken out flat. Carefully loosen skin, but do not remove. Stuff butter mixture between meat and skin, spreading mixture as evenly as possible. Preheat gas barbecue to medium. Turn off centre or left burner. Place chicken, breast-side down, on greased grill over drip pan on unlit side. Close lid. Cook for 35 minutes. Carefully turn chicken over. Cook for about 45 minutes until meat thermometer inserted in thigh reads 180°F (82°C). Remove chicken from heat. Cover with foil. Let stand for 15 minutes. Cut into serving-size portions. Serves 4 to 6.

1 serving: 504 Calories; 32.8 g Total Fat (15.1 g Mono, 6.1 g Poly, 8.5 g Sat); 155 mg Cholesterol; 1 g Carbohydrate; trace Fibre; 48 g Protein; 400 mg Sodium

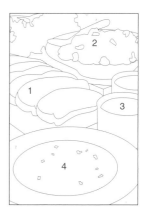

1. Feta Herb Bread, page 43
2. Seashell Pasta Salad, page 61
3. Fresh Herb Tea, page 41
4. Spicy Yam Soup, page 64

Props Courtesy Of: Casa Bugatti
Island Pottery Inc.

Green Peppercorn Chicken

Rich, peppery cream sauce over tender chicken.

Hard margarine (or butter)	2 tbsp.	30 mL
Cooking oil	2 tsp.	10 mL
Boneless, skinless chicken breast halves	4	4
(about 4 – 6 oz., 113 – 170 g, each)		
All-purpose flour	1 tbsp.	15 mL
Prepared chicken broth	1 cup	250 mL
Whole green peppercorns, drained	1 1/2 tbsp.	25 mL
Half-and-half cream	3 tbsp.	50 mL

Heat margarine and cooking oil in large frying pan on medium. Add chicken breast halves. Cook for about 10 minutes per side, depending on thickness, until no longer pink inside. Remove chicken to serving dish. Cover to keep warm. Set aside.

Add flour to same frying pan. Heat and stir for 2 minutes.

Slowly add broth, stirring constantly and scraping any brown bits from bottom of pan. Heat and stir for about 5 minutes until boiling and thickened.

Add peppercorns and cream. Heat and stir until hot. Drizzle sauce over chicken breast halves. Serves 4.

1 serving: 262 Calories; 12 g Total Fat (6.2 g Mono, 1.9 g Poly, 2.8 g Sat); 85 mg Cholesterol; 3 g Carbohydrate; trace Fibre; 34 g Protein; 278 mg Sodium

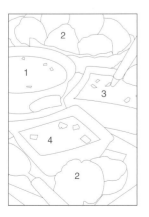

1. Indonesian Chicken Soup, page 68
2. Sun-Dried Tomato Muffins, page 45
3. Curried Chicken Soup, page 66
4. Vegetable Soup, page 67

Props Courtesy Of: Casa Bugatti
                     Cherison Enterprises Inc.
                     Danesco Inc.

Lemon Grass Chicken

Delicate lemon grass, creamy coconut and crunchy nuts transform ordinary chicken into a flavourful dish!

Sprigs of fresh cilantro (or parsley)	1/4 cup	60 mL
Small fresh red chili with seeds (or 1 – 2 tsp., 5 – 10 mL, dried crushed chilies)	1	1
Garlic cloves	2	2
Finely grated, peeled gingerroot	1 tsp.	5 mL
Cooking oil	1 tbsp.	15 mL
Lime juice	1 tbsp.	15 mL
Lemon grass, bulb only (root and stalk removed), cut into 3 equal pieces	1	1
Can of coconut milk	14 oz.	398 mL
Water	1/3 cup	75 mL
Brown sugar, packed	2 tsp.	10 mL
Fish sauce	2 tsp.	10 mL
Boneless, skinless chicken thighs (or breast halves), cut into 1 inch (2.5 cm) pieces	1 lb.	454 g
Fresh bean sprouts (about 3 oz., 85 g)	1 cup	250 mL
Lime juice	2 tbsp.	30 mL
Chopped fresh cilantro (or parsley)	3 tbsp.	50 mL
Cashews (or sliced almonds), toasted (see Tip, page 33)	3 tbsp.	50 mL

Process first 6 ingredients in blender until smooth paste.

Heat wok or large frying pan on medium until hot. Add cilantro mixture and lemon grass. Stir-fry for 1 to 2 minutes until fragrant. Add next 4 ingredients. Stir. Bring to a gentle boil.

Add chicken. Reduce heat to medium-low. Simmer, uncovered, for 20 to 25 minutes, stirring occasionally, until chicken is no longer pink inside and sauce is slightly thickened. Remove from heat.

Add bean sprouts and lime juice. Stir. Transfer to serving dish. Remove and discard lemon grass bulb.

Sprinkle with cilantro and cashews. Serves 4.

1 serving: 435 Calories; 33 g Total Fat (6.6 g Mono, 3.3 g Poly, 20.4 g Sat); 94 mg Cholesterol; 12 g Carbohydrate; 1 g Fibre; 26 g Protein; 195 mg Sodium

Pictured on page 90.

Chicken Burgers

Not your ordinary burger! This tasty combination
of flavours will have your family asking for more.

Red medium pepper, seeds and ribs removed, quartered	1	1
Fine dry bread crumbs	1/3 cup	75 mL
Grated Parmesan cheese	1/3 cup	75 mL
Chopped fresh parsley	1/4 cup	60 mL
Liquid honey	1 tbsp.	15 mL
Large egg	1	1
Finely grated lemon zest	1 tsp.	5 mL
Ground cinnamon	1/2 tsp.	2 mL
Lemon pepper	1/2 tsp.	2 mL
Lean ground chicken	1 lb.	454 g
Goat (chèvre) cheese, cut up	4 oz.	113 g
Kaiser rolls, split and toasted	4	4
Fresh spinach, stems removed, lightly packed	1 cup	250 mL

Preheat electric grill for 5 minutes or gas barbecue to medium-high. Cook pepper on greased grill (or broil in oven), skin-side down, for 10 to 12 minutes until skin is blackened and blistered. Transfer to small bowl. Cover with plastic wrap. Let sweat for about 15 minutes until cool enough to handle. Peel and discard skin. Cut into thin strips. Set aside.

Combine next 8 ingredients in large bowl. Add ground chicken. Mix well. Divide and shape into 4 equal patties to fit kaiser rolls. Cook patties on same greased grill for about 5 minutes per side until chicken is no longer pink. Do not overcook.

Divide and spread goat cheese on both cut sides of each roll. Divide and layer red pepper on bottom half of each roll. Top each with 1 chicken patty. Divide and layer spinach over chicken patties. Cover with top halves of rolls. Makes 4 burgers.

1 burger: 535 Calories; 19 g Total Fat (5.1 g Mono, 2.5 g Poly, 9.3 g Sat); 163 mg Cholesterol; 46 g Carbohydrate; 2 g Fibre; 43 g Protein; 819 mg Sodium

Pictured on page 89.

Paré Pointer
Laugh lots and lots and when you get old your wrinkles will be in the right place.

Jazz 'N' Roll Chicken

Lemon and chive cream cheese rolled inside tender chicken breasts. Jazzy
spiced bread crumbs coat the outside. A wonderful dish for company.

Block of cream cheese, softened	4 oz.	125 g
Bacon slices, cooked crisp and crumbled	2	2
Chopped fresh chives (or green onion)	1 1/2 tbsp.	25 mL
Finely grated lemon zest	1/4 tsp.	1 mL
Boneless, skinless chicken breast halves (about 4 – 6 oz., 113 – 170 g, each)	4	4
Jean's Jazz, page 14, sprinkle (optional)		
All-purpose flour	2 tbsp.	30 mL
Large egg	1	1
Fine dry bread crumbs	3/4 cup	175 mL
Jean's Jazz, page 14	1 1/2 tbsp.	25 mL
Cooking oil	2 tbsp.	30 mL

Beat first 4 ingredients in small bowl.

Place 1 chicken breast half between 2 sheets of waxed paper. Pound with mallet or rolling pin to 1/4 inch (6 mm) thickness. Remove top layer of waxed paper. Sprinkle chicken with Jean's Jazz. Repeat with remaining chicken breast halves and first amount of Jean's Jazz. Divide and spread cream cheese mixture on each chicken breast half leaving 1/2 inch (12 mm) at edges. Roll up from short side, jelly roll-style, to enclose filling. Secure with wooden picks.

Measure flour onto sheet of waxed paper.

Beat egg with fork in small bowl.

Combine bread crumbs and second amount of Jean's Jazz in medium bowl. Dredge each chicken roll in flour. Dip into egg. Coat well in crumb mixture.

Heat cooking oil in large frying pan on medium. Add chicken rolls. Cook for 5 to 10 minutes, turning occasionally, until golden. Place on greased baking sheet. Cook in 350°F (175°C) oven for about 15 minutes until chicken is no longer pink inside and lightly browned. Remove wooden picks. Serves 4.

1 serving: 468 Calories; 24.4 g Total Fat (9.4 g Mono, 3.8 g Poly, 9.2 g Sat); 172 mg Cholesterol; 21 g Carbohydrate; 1 g Fibre; 40 g Protein; 1234 mg Sodium

Olive-Stuffed Chicken

Golden brown chicken with a Moroccan flair. Moist rice stuffing with mint, honey and olives. A perfect combination.

Moroccan Spice Rub, page 21	2 tbsp.	30 mL
Salt	1/2 tsp.	2 mL
Whole roasting chicken	3 lbs.	1.4 kg
Olive (or cooking) oil	1 tbsp.	15 mL
OLIVE STUFFING		
Olive (or cooking) oil	1 tbsp.	15 mL
Finely chopped onion	1/2 cup	125 mL
Finely chopped celery rib	1/4 cup	60 mL
Finely chopped carrot	1/4 cup	60 mL
Dry white (or alcohol-free) wine	1/3 cup	75 mL
Cooked long grain white rice (3/4 cup, 175 mL, uncooked)	1 1/2 cups	375 mL
Chopped pitted large green olives	1/3 cup	75 mL
Chopped fresh mint leaves (or 2 1/4 tsp., 11 mL, dried)	3 tbsp.	50 mL
Liquid honey	2 tbsp.	30 mL
Finely grated orange zest	1 tsp.	5 mL

Combine Moroccan Spice Rub and salt in small bowl.

Rub chicken with olive oil. Place in extra-large bowl. Sprinkle spice mixture over chicken. Cover. Chill for 6 hours.

Olive Stuffing: Heat olive oil in large frying pan on medium. Add onion, celery and carrot. Cook for 5 to 10 minutes, stirring often, until vegetables are softened. Add wine. Heat and stir until wine is almost evaporated. Remove from heat.

Add remaining 5 ingredients. Stir well. Stuff chicken with rice mixture. Tie legs together with butcher's string. Tie wings to body. Place on greased wire rack set in large roasting pan. Cover. Cook in 350°F (175°C) oven for about 1 3/4 hours until meat thermometer inserted in thigh reads 185°F (85°C). Remove stuffing to small bowl. Makes 3 cups (750 mL) stuffing. Cut chicken into serving-size portions. Serves 4.

1 serving of chicken with 3/4 cup (175 mL) stuffing: 573 Calories; 27.3 g Total Fat (13.5 g Mono, 4.8 g Poly, 6.3 g Sat); 118 mg Cholesterol; 38 g Carbohydrate; 2 g Fibre; 40 g Protein; 1167 mg Sodium

Beef And Lemon Grass

Tender-crisp strips of red pepper and green onion add colour and flavour
to this lightly spiced beef and asparagus stir-fry.

Cooking oil	1 tbsp.	15 mL
Lemon grass, bulb only (root and stalk removed), chopped finely	1	1
Garlic clove, minced (or 1/4 tsp., 1 mL, powder)	1	1
Ground ginger	1 tsp.	5 mL
Chili paste (sambal oelek)	1/2 – 1 tsp.	2 – 5 mL
Pepper	1/4 tsp.	1 mL
Top sirloin steak, sliced thinly	3/4 lb.	340 g
Water	3 tbsp.	50 mL
Hoisin sauce	2 tbsp.	30 mL
Oyster sauce	1 tbsp.	15 mL
Cornstarch	2 tsp.	10 mL
Cooking oil	2 tsp.	10 mL
Cooking oil	2 tsp.	10 mL
Red medium pepper, sliced thinly	1	1
Fresh asparagus, trimmed of tough ends and cut into 1 inch (2.5 cm) pieces	8 oz.	225 g
Green onions, cut into 1 inch (2.5 cm) pieces	6	6

Combine first 6 ingredients in medium bowl.

Add beef. Toss until coated. Cover. Marinate in refrigerator for at least 6 hours or overnight.

Measure next 4 ingredients into small bowl. Stir. Set aside.

Heat wok or large frying pan on medium-high until very hot. Add second amount of cooking oil. Add beef with marinade. Stir-fry until beef is just tender. Transfer to separate small bowl.

Heat third amount of cooking oil in same wok. Add red pepper, asparagus and green onion. Stir-fry for 1 minute. Stir hoisin sauce mixture. Add to vegetables. Add beef mixture. Stir-fry for 2 to 3 minutes until vegetables are tender-crisp. Makes 3 cups (750 mL). Serves 3.

1 serving: 358 Calories; 21.3 g Total Fat (10.7 g Mono, 3.8 g Poly, 4.9 g Sat); 56 mg Cholesterol; 18 g Carbohydrate; 2 g Fibre; 24 g Protein; 759 mg Sodium

West Indies Beef

A one-dish meal with rice and exceptionally tender, spicy beef.

All-purpose flour	1/3 cup	75 mL
Seasoned Salt, page 14	1 tsp.	5 mL
Paprika	1 tsp.	5 mL
Pepper	1/2 tsp.	2 mL
Inside round (or boneless blade) steak, trimmed of fat, cut into 3/4 inch (2 cm) cubes	2 lbs.	900 g
Cooking oil	2 tbsp.	30 mL
Chopped onion	1 1/2 cups	375 mL
Garlic cloves, minced (or 1/2 tsp., 2 mL, powder)	2	2
Water	2 tbsp.	30 mL
Chopped tomato	2 cups	500 mL
Chopped green pepper	1 cup	250 mL
Finely grated, peeled gingerroot (or 1 tsp., 5 mL, ground ginger)	1 tbsp.	15 mL
Ground cumin	1/2 tsp.	2 mL
Cayenne pepper	1/4 tsp.	1 mL
Long grain white rice	1 cup	250 mL
Water	2 1/2 cups	625 mL
Salt	1 tsp.	5 mL

Measure first 4 ingredients into medium bowl. Stir. Add beef. Toss until coated. Heat cooking oil in large frying pan on medium-high. Cook beef mixture, in 3 batches, until beef is browned on all sides. Transfer to ungreased 2 1/2 quart (2.5 L) casserole, reserving any brown bits and cooking oil in pan.

Add onion, garlic and first amount of water to same frying pan. Heat and stir for about 5 minutes, scraping brown bits from bottom of pan, until onion is just softened. Add to beef.

Add next 5 ingredients. Stir. Cover. Bake in 325°F (160°C) oven for about 1 1/2 hours until beef is tender.

Combine remaining 3 ingredients in medium saucepan. Bring to a boil on medium. Reduce heat to medium-low. Simmer, uncovered, for about 10 minutes, without stirring, until partially cooked. Do not drain. Pour rice mixture into beef mixture. Stir. Cover. Bake for about 30 minutes until rice is tender. Makes 6 2/3 cups (1.65 L). Serves 6.

1 serving: 438 Calories; 13.1 g Total Fat (5.9 g Mono, 2 g Poly, 3.1 g Sat); 70 mg Cholesterol; 40 g Carbohydrate; 2 g Fibre; 38 g Protein; 792 mg Sodium

Sirloin Strips

A bit of tomato sauce coats every bite. Good served with egg noodles.

Cooking oil	2 tsp.	10 mL
Medium onion, cut into 8 wedges	1	1
Red medium pepper, seeds and ribs removed, cut into 1 inch (2.5 cm) pieces	1	1
Garlic cloves, minced (or 1/2 tsp., 2 mL, powder)	2	2
Can of diced tomatoes (with juice)	14 oz.	398 mL
Dry red (or alcohol-free) wine	1/3 cup	75 mL
Beef bouillon powder	1 tsp.	5 mL
All-purpose flour	1 1/2 tbsp.	25 mL
Cornstarch	4 tsp.	20 mL
Salt	1/4 tsp.	1 mL
Pepper	1/4 tsp.	1 mL
Top sirloin steak, cut into thin 4 inch (10 cm) strips	1 lb.	454 g
Cooking oil	1 tbsp.	15 mL
Chopped fresh basil (see Note)	2 tsp.	10 mL
Chopped fresh oregano (see Note)	2 tsp.	10 mL
Chopped fresh rosemary (see Note)	1/2 tsp.	2 mL
Chopped fresh spinach, packed	2 cups	500 mL

Heat first amount of cooking oil in large saucepan on medium. Add onion and red pepper. Cook for about 5 minutes, stirring often, until onion is just softened. Add garlic. Heat and stir for 1 to 2 minutes until fragrant.

Add tomatoes with juice, wine and bouillon powder. Stir. Bring to a boil. Reduce heat to medium-low. Cover. Simmer for 20 minutes, stirring occasionally. Remove from heat.

Measure next 4 ingredients into medium bowl. Stir. Add beef. Toss until coated.

Heat second amount of cooking oil in large frying pan on medium-high. Add beef mixture. Cook for about 5 minutes until beef is browned. Add tomato mixture. Heat and stir for about 5 minutes, scraping any brown bits from bottom of pan, until boiling.

Add basil, oregano and rosemary. Stir. Reduce heat to low. Cover. Simmer for about 10 minutes, stirring occasionally, until sauce is thickened.

(continued on next page)

Add spinach. Heat and stir for about 1 minute until wilted. Makes 5 cups (1.25 L). Serves 6.

1 serving: 217 Calories; 11 g Total Fat (5.2 g Mono, 1.6 g Poly, 3 g Sat); 38 mg Cholesterol; 11 g Carbohydrate; 2 g Fibre; 17 g Protein; 366 mg Sodium

Pictured on page 107.

Note: Omit fresh herbs. Substitute 1/2 tsp. (2 mL) dried basil, 1/2 tsp. (2 mL) dried whole oregano and 1/8 tsp. (0.5 mL) ground rosemary when adding diced tomatoes to saucepan. Dried herbs should be cooked longer than fresh herbs to release flavour. Add fresh herbs near end of cooking time for best flavour.

Minted Beef Skewers

Tender beef with an Asian flair. Serve with rice and enjoy!

Finely chopped onion	1/2 cup	125 mL
Chopped fresh mint leaves	1/3 cup	75 mL
Fish sauce	3 tbsp.	50 mL
Finely chopped lemon grass, bulb only (root and stalk removed)	2 tbsp.	30 mL
Cooking (or peanut) oil	2 tbsp.	30 mL
Sweet (or regular) chili sauce	2 tbsp.	30 mL
Curry powder	1 tbsp.	15 mL
Coarse ground pepper	2 tsp.	10 mL
Finely grated, peeled gingerroot	2 tsp.	10 mL
Garlic cloves, minced (or 1/2 tsp., 2 mL, powder)	2	2
Top sirloin steak, cut into 3/4 inch (2 cm) cubes	1 1/2 lbs.	680 g
Bamboo skewers (8 inch, 20 cm, length), soaked in water for 10 minutes	12	12

Combine first 10 ingredients in medium bowl.

Add beef. Stir until coated. Cover. Marinate in refrigerator for at least 8 hours or overnight.

Thread beef onto skewers. Preheat electric grill for 5 minutes or gas barbecue to medium-high. Cook beef on greased grill (or broil in oven) for 8 to 10 minutes, turning occasionally, until desired doneness. Makes 12 beef skewers.

1 beef skewer: 125 Calories; 7.5 g Total Fat (3.5 g Mono, 0.9 g Poly, 2.2 g Sat); 28 mg Cholesterol; 3 g Carbohydrate; trace Fibre; 12 g Protein; 331 mg Sodium

Beef Biryani

An aromatic, Indian-inspired dish. Tender beef in a seasoned rice base.
Toasted almonds add a satisfying crunch.

Plain yogurt	1/2 cup	125 mL
Chili powder	1 1/2 tsp.	7 mL
Ground cumin	1 1/2 tsp.	7 mL
Ground coriander	1 1/2 tsp.	7 mL
Beef stew meat, cut into 1/2 inch (12 mm) cubes	1/2 lb.	225 g
Basmati (or long grain) white rice	2 cups	500 mL
Water		
Cooking oil	2 tbsp.	30 mL
Medium onions, sliced thinly (about 2 cups, 500 mL)	2	2
Prepared beef broth	1 cup	250 mL
Ground cumin	1 tsp.	5 mL
Ground coriander	1 tsp.	5 mL
Ground ginger	1 tsp.	5 mL
Chili powder	1 tsp.	5 mL
Whole green cardamom, bruised (see Tip, page 83)	6	6
Cinnamon stick (4 inches, 10 cm)	1	1
Salt	3/4 tsp.	4 mL
Prepared beef broth	2 cups	500 mL
Frozen peas	1 cup	250 mL
Slivered almonds, toasted (see Tip, page 33)	1 cup	250 mL
Medium tomatoes, quartered, seeds removed, chopped	2	2
Currants	2/3 cup	150 mL
Chopped fresh cilantro, parsley or mint (optional)	2 tbsp.	30 mL

(continued on next page)

Combine first 4 ingredients in medium bowl.

Add beef. Stir. Cover. Chill for 30 minutes to blend flavours.

Measure rice into medium bowl. Cover with water. Let stand for 30 minutes. Drain. Set aside.

Heat cooking oil in large pot or Dutch oven on medium-low. Add onion. Cook for 15 to 20 minutes, stirring often, until caramelized.

Add beef mixture and next 8 ingredients. Stir. Bring to a boil on medium. Reduce heat to medium-low. Cover. Simmer for about 1 1/2 hours, stirring occasionally, until beef is tender. Remove and discard cardamom and cinnamon stick.

Add rice and second amount of broth. Stir. Bring to a boil on medium. Reduce heat to medium-low. Cover. Simmer for about 15 minutes, without stirring, until rice is tender.

Add next 4 ingredients. Stir. Cover. Cook for about 5 minutes until heated through. Transfer to serving dish.

Sprinkle with cilantro, parsley or mint. Makes 10 cups (2.5 L). Serves 6.

1 serving: 600 Calories; 21.7 g Total Fat (12.3 g Mono, 4.3 g Poly, 3.3 g Sat); 22 mg Cholesterol; 81 g Carbohydrate; 6 g Fibre; 23 g Protein; 504 mg Sodium

 To bruise cardamom, hit cardamom pods with a mallet or flat side of a wide knife to "bruise" or crack them slightly open.

Paré Pointer
The best plastic surgery is simply cutting up your credit cards.

Beef Madras Curry

Wonderful curry flavour creates a gentle heat, while coconut adds texture and fragrance. Lots of sauce to serve over rice or couscous.

Medium unsweetened coconut	1 cup	250 mL
Medium tomatoes, peeled (see Tip, page 63) and coarsely chopped	4	4
Lemon juice	2 tbsp.	30 mL
Brown mustard seed	2 tbsp.	30 mL
Finely grated, peeled gingerroot	1 tbsp.	15 mL
Cooking oil	1 tbsp.	15 mL
Thinly sliced onion	2 cups	500 mL
Garlic cloves, minced (or 3/4 tsp., 4 mL, powder)	3	3
Ground cumin	2 tsp.	10 mL
Ground coriander	2 tsp.	10 mL
Paprika	2 tsp.	10 mL
Turmeric	1 tsp.	5 mL
Dried crushed chilies	1 tsp.	5 mL
Salt	1/2 tsp.	2 mL
Boneless beef blade steak, trimmed of fat, cut into 3/4 inch (2 cm) cubes	2 lbs.	900 g
Prepared beef broth	2/3 cup	150 mL
Liquid beef bouillon concentrate (such as Bovril)	1 1/2 tsp.	7 mL

Process first 5 ingredients in blender or food processor until almost smooth. Set aside.

Heat cooking oil in large pot or Dutch oven on medium. Add onion. Cook for 5 to 10 minutes, stirring often, until softened.

Add next 7 ingredients. Heat and stir for 1 to 2 minutes until fragrant.

Add beef. Stir until coated. Add broth, bouillon concentrate and coconut mixture. Stir. Bring to a boil. Reduce heat to low. Cover. Simmer for 1 1/2 hours, stirring occasionally. Increase heat to medium-low. Simmer, uncovered, for 20 to 30 minutes, stirring occasionally, until sauce is thickened and beef is tender. Makes about 6 cups (1.5 L). Serves 8.

1 serving: 314 Calories; 19.1 g Total Fat (5.7 g Mono, 1.2 g Poly, 10.1 g Sat); 60 mg Cholesterol; 13 g Carbohydrate; 3 g Fibre; 25 g Protein; 434 mg Sodium

Pictured on page 143.

Coconut Fish Curry

Coconut and curry with tender white fish.

Medium unsweetened coconut	2/3 cup	150 mL
Cumin seed	2 tsp.	10 mL
Coriander seed	2 tsp.	10 mL
Ground ginger	1 tsp.	5 mL
Turmeric	1/2 tsp.	2 mL
Dried crushed chilies	1/2 tsp.	2 mL
Cooking oil	1 tbsp.	15 mL
Chopped onion	1 1/2 cups	375 mL
Garlic cloves, minced	2	2
Whole green cardamom, bruised (see Tip, page 83)	8	8
Medium tomatoes, peeled (see Tip, page 63) and chopped	2	2
Can of coconut milk	14 oz.	398 mL
Prepared chicken broth	1/2 cup	125 mL
Brown sugar, packed	2 tsp.	10 mL
Salt	1/2 tsp.	2 mL
Skinless halibut fillets (or other mild white fish), bones removed, cut into 1 inch (2.5 cm) cubes	1 1/2 lbs.	680 g

Process first 6 ingredients in blender or food processor until seeds are finely crushed. Heat medium frying pan on medium until hot. Add coconut mixture. Cook for about 5 minutes, stirring constantly, until coconut is fragrant and lightly browned. Transfer to small bowl. Set aside.

Heat cooking oil in large saucepan on medium. Add onion. Cook for 5 to 10 minutes, stirring often, until softened.

Add garlic and cardamom. Heat and stir for 1 to 2 minutes until fragrant.

Add next 5 ingredients. Stir. Add coconut mixture. Stir well. Bring to a boil. Reduce heat to medium-low. Simmer, uncovered, for 10 to 15 minutes, stirring occasionally, until thickened.

Add halibut. Stir. Cover. Simmer, without stirring, for about 10 minutes until halibut is tender. Serves 6.

1 serving: 382 Calories; 25.9 g Total Fat (3.2 g Mono, 2 g Poly, 18.7 g Sat); 36 mg Cholesterol; 13 g Carbohydrate; 2 g Fibre; 27 g Protein; 349 mg Sodium

Pictured on page 108.

Mussels And Pasta Shells

A savoury seafood dish. If you prefer, mussel shells can be removed from the sauce before serving.

Fresh mussels, scrubbed and "beards" removed (about 26)	3 1/4 lbs.	1.5 kg
Olive (or cooking) oil	1 tsp.	5 mL
Finely chopped onion	1/2 cup	125 mL
Garlic clove, minced (or 1/4 tsp., 1 mL, powder)	1	1
Dry red (or alcohol-free) wine	1/4 cup	60 mL
Can of diced tomatoes (with juice)	14 oz.	398 mL
Tomato paste (see Tip, page 87)	2 1/2 tbsp.	37 mL
Chopped fresh basil, packed (or 1 1/2 tsp., 7 mL, dried)	2 tbsp.	30 mL
Chopped fresh parsley (or 3/4 tsp., 4 mL, flakes)	1 tbsp.	15 mL
Bay leaf	1	1
Lemon juice	1/2 tsp.	2 mL
Granulated sugar	1/4 tsp.	1 mL
Dried crushed chilies	1/16 tsp.	0.5 mL
Pepper, sprinkle		
Large shell pasta (about 5 oz., 140 g)	2 cups	500 mL
Boiling water		
Salt		

Put mussels into medium bowl. Lightly tap any that are opened 1/4 inch (6 mm) or more. Discard any that do not close.

Heat olive oil in large saucepan on medium. Add onion. Cook for 5 to 10 minutes, stirring often, until softened. Add garlic. Heat and stir for 1 to 2 minutes until fragrant.

Add wine. Stir. Bring to a boil. Add mussels. Reduce heat to medium-low. Cover. Simmer for about 3 minutes, without stirring, until mussels open. Remove to large bowl using slotted spoon. Reserve liquid in saucepan. Discard any unopened mussels. Cover opened mussels to keep warm.

Add next 9 ingredients to liquid in saucepan. Stir. Increase heat to medium. Bring to a boil. Reduce heat to medium-low. Cover. Simmer for 10 minutes, stirring occasionally. Remove from heat. Remove and discard bay leaf. Cover to keep warm.

(continued on next page)

Cook pasta shells in boiling water and salt in large uncovered pot or Dutch oven for 10 to 12 minutes, stirring occasionally, until tender but firm. Drain. Add to sauce. Add mussels. Toss until pasta is coated. Serves 2.

1 serving: 562 Calories; 8.8 g Total Fat (3 g Mono, 2.2 g Poly, 1.5 g Sat); 58 mg Cholesterol; 78 g Carbohydrate; 5 g Fibre; 37 g Protein; 948 mg Sodium

Pictured on page 108.

Halibut Skewers

Delicate citrus and herb flavours. Serve with your favourite vegetable skewers.

Orange juice	1 cup	250 mL
Lemon juice	2 tbsp.	30 mL
Finely grated lemon zest	1 tsp.	5 mL
Garlic clove, minced (or 1/4 tsp., 1 mL, powder)	1	1
Sprigs of fresh savory (about 4 inches, 10 cm, each)	4	4
Fresh savory, minced	1 tsp.	5 mL
Salt	1/2 tsp.	2 mL
Pepper	1/2 tsp.	2 mL
Skinless halibut fillets (or other mild white fish), bones removed, cut into 1 inch (2.5 cm) cubes	1 1/2 lbs.	680 g
Bamboo skewers (8 inch, 20 cm, length), soaked in water for 10 minutes	6	6

Measure first 8 ingredients into large bowl. Stir.

Add halibut. Stir gently until coated. Cover. Marinate in refrigerator for up to 60 minutes, stirring occasionally. Remove savory sprigs.

Thread halibut onto skewers. Brush with orange juice mixture. Preheat electric grill for 5 minutes or gas barbecue to medium. Cook skewers on greased grill (or broil in oven) for about 7 minutes, turning several times, until firm and no longer opaque. Do not overcook. Makes 6 halibut skewers.

1 halibut skewer: 147 Calories; 2.7 g Total Fat (0.9 g Mono, 1 g Poly, 0.4 g Sat); 36 mg Cholesterol; 5 g Carbohydrate; trace Fibre; 24 g Protein; 260 mg Sodium

 If a recipe calls for less than an entire can of tomato paste, freeze can for 30 minutes. Open both ends and push contents through one end. Slice off only what you need. Freeze remaining paste in plastic wrap for future use.

Curry Crumbed Red Snapper

Snapper coated in crunchy poppy seeds and curry.
An alternative to chicken strips.

Cornflakes cereal	1 1/2 cups	375 mL
Curry powder	2 1/4 tsp.	11 mL
Poppy seeds	1 1/2 tsp.	7 mL
Paprika	1 tsp.	5 mL
Garlic salt	1/2 tsp.	2 mL
Large eggs	2	2
All-purpose flour	2 tbsp.	30 mL
Skinless red snapper fillets, bones removed, cut into 1 inch (2.5 cm) wide strips	1 lb.	454 g
Cooking oil	3 tbsp.	50 mL

Process cereal in blender or food processor until fine crumbs. Transfer to small bowl. Add next 4 ingredients. Stir.

Beat eggs with fork in separate small bowl. Measure flour onto sheet of waxed paper. Dredge each strip of snapper in flour. Dip into egg. Coat well in crumb mixture. Place strips on ungreased baking sheet. Chill for 30 minutes.

Heat 1 1/2 tbsp. (25 mL) cooking oil in large frying pan on medium-low. Cook 1/2 of snapper strips for 3 to 4 minutes per side, depending on thickness, until fish flakes easily with fork. Cover to keep warm. Repeat with remaining cooking oil and strips. Serve immediately. Serves 4.

1 serving: 306 Calories; 15.2 g Total Fat (7.4 g Mono, 4.3 g Poly, 1.9 g Sat); 150 mg Cholesterol; 13 g Carbohydrate; 1 g Fibre; 28 g Protein; 350 mg Sodium

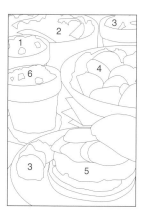

1. Tomato Relish, page 133
2. Mushroom Broccoli Salad, page 50
3. Bread And Butter Pickles, page 129
4. Potato Mint Salad, page 59
5. Chicken Burgers, page 75
6. Corn Relish, page 134

Props Courtesy Of: Danesco Inc.

Cajun Garlic Shrimp

Mildly spiced, tender shrimp. Add more spice mix for more bite.

Olive (or cooking) oil	1 tbsp.	15 mL
Fresh medium shrimp, peeled and deveined (about 35)	1 lb.	454 g
Medium onion, cut into thin wedges	1	1
Garlic clove, minced (or 1/4 tsp., 1 mL, powder)	1	1
Cajun Spice Mix, page 21	1 1/2 – 2 tsp.	7 – 10 mL
Dry white (or alcohol-free) wine	1/4 cup	60 mL
Evaporated milk (or half-and-half cream)	1/2 cup	125 mL
Chopped fresh parsley (or 1 1/2 tsp., 7 mL, flakes)	2 tbsp.	30 mL

Heat olive oil in large frying pan on medium. Add shrimp. Cook for 2 to 3 minutes, stirring constantly, until shrimp just start to turn pink. Transfer shrimp to large bowl. Reserve olive oil in pan.

Heat reserved olive oil on medium. Add onion. Cook for 5 to 10 minutes, stirring often, until softened.

Add garlic and spice mix. Heat and stir for 1 to 2 minutes until fragrant.

Add wine. Heat and stir until liquid is almost evaporated.

Add evaporated milk and parsley. Heat and stir until slightly thickened. Return shrimp to pan. Stir until just heated through. Do not overcook. Serves 4.

1 serving: 192 Calories; 7.7 g Total Fat (3.6 g Mono, 1 g Poly, 2.3 g Sat); 139 mg Cholesterol; 7 g Carbohydrate; 1 g Fibre; 20 g Protein; 214 mg Sodium

Pictured on page 108.

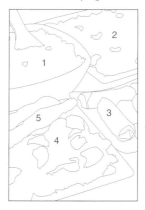

1. Curry Fried Rice, page 112
2. Lemon Grass Chicken, page 74
3. Beef Spring Rolls, page 22
4. Oriental Pork Salad, page 60
5. Twisted Chopsticks, page 24

Props Courtesy Of: Cherison Enterprises Inc.

Entrées

Salmon Dill Pasta

Slightly sweet sauce with tender, mild salmon, fresh dill and lemon.

Maple (or maple-flavoured) syrup	2 tbsp.	30 mL
Marmalade (your favourite)	1 tbsp.	15 mL
Chopped fresh dill (or 3/4 tsp., 4 mL, dill weed)	1 tbsp.	15 mL
Olive (or cooking) oil	2 tsp.	10 mL
Salt	1/4 tsp.	1 mL
Skinless salmon fillet, bones removed	1/2 lb.	225 g
Medium bow (or other) pasta (about 4 oz., 113 g)	1 1/2 cups	375 mL
Boiling water	8 cups	2 L
Salt	1 tsp.	5 mL
Hard margarine (or butter)	2 tbsp.	30 mL
Finely chopped red onion	1/2 cup	125 mL
All-purpose flour	2 tbsp.	30 mL
Milk	1 1/2 cups	375 mL
Chopped fresh dill (or 3/4 tsp., 4 mL, dill weed)	1 tbsp.	15 mL
Finely grated lemon zest	1/2 tsp.	2 mL
Salt, sprinkle		
Pepper	1/4 tsp.	1 mL

Combine first 5 ingredients in small bowl.

Brush maple syrup mixture over both sides of salmon. Place on sheet of greased heavy-duty foil. Preheat electric grill for 5 minutes or gas barbecue to medium. Cook salmon (on foil) on greased grill for 3 to 4 minutes per side, depending on thickness, until salmon flakes easily with fork. Remove to serving dish. Flake salmon with fork into small pieces. Set aside.

Cook pasta in boiling water and salt in large uncovered pot or Dutch oven for 12 to 15 minutes, stirring occasionally, until tender but firm. Drain well. Return to same pot. Cover to keep warm.

Melt margarine in medium saucepan on medium. Add onion. Cook for 5 to 10 minutes, stirring often, until softened. Add flour. Heat and stir for about 1 minute until smooth. Slowly add milk, stirring constantly, until boiling and thickened.

Add remaining 4 ingredients. Stir. Pour over pasta. Toss until coated. Add salmon. Toss. Makes 4 cups (1 L). Serves 4.

1 serving: 373 Calories; 13.3 g Total Fat (7 g Mono, 2.5 g Poly, 2.8 g Sat); 35 mg Cholesterol; 44 g Carbohydrate; 1 g Fibre; 19 g Protein; 296 mg Sodium

Stuffed Pork Loin

This elegant roast is sure to impress your guests. Try it glazed with
Spiced Peach Topping, page 128.

SAGE AND APRICOT STUFFING

Fresh white bread cubes (crusts removed), about 4 slices	3 cups	750 mL
Finely chopped onion	2/3 cup	150 mL
Finely chopped dried apricots	1/2 cup	125 mL
Chopped fresh sage (or 1 1/2 tsp., 7 mL, dried)	2 tbsp.	30 mL
Orange marmalade	2 tbsp.	30 mL
Dry mustard	1 tsp.	5 mL
Salt	1/4 tsp.	1 mL
Pepper	1/2 tsp.	2 mL
Lean boneless pork loin (1 piece)	4 1/2 lbs.	2 kg
Cooking oil	2 tsp.	10 mL
Salt, sprinkle		

Sage And Apricot Stuffing: Spread bread cubes in single layer on ungreased baking sheet. Bake in 250°F (120°C) oven for about 15 minutes, stirring occasionally, until dried. Transfer to large bowl.

Add next 7 ingredients. Stir well. Makes 3 1/3 cups (825 mL) stuffing.

Cut pork loin almost in half lengthwise, not quite through to other side. Press open to flatten. Place between 2 pieces of plastic wrap. Pound with mallet or rolling pin to even 3/4 inch (2 cm) thickness. Remove and discard plastic wrap. Spoon stuffing lengthwise along centre of pork. Roll, from long side, up and over stuffing to enclose. Tie with butcher's string or secure with metal skewers.

Brush pork with cooking oil. Sprinkle with salt. Place, seam-side down, on greased wire rack set in medium roasting pan. Cover. Cook in 325°F (160°C) oven for 1 1/2 to 2 hours until meat thermometer inserted into thickest part of pork (not stuffing) reads 155°F (68°C), or until desired doneness. Remove from oven. Cover with foil. Let stand for 10 minutes. Internal temperature should rise to at least 160°F (70°C). Remove butcher's string. Serves 18.

1 serving: 202 Calories; 7.3 g Total Fat (3.4 g Mono, 0.9 g Poly, 2.3 g Sat); 67 mg Cholesterol; 8 g Carbohydrate; trace Fibre; 25 g Protein; 127 mg Sodium

Pictured on page 126.

Roasted Pepper Pork

Baked pork tenderloin with colourful red pepper, ricotta and herb filling.
A wonderful dish to serve when you have guests for dinner!

Pork tenderloin, trimmed of fat	1 lb.	454 g
Dijon mustard (with whole seeds)	2 tbsp.	30 mL
Roasted red pepper, drained and blotted dry, cut into thin strips	1/2 cup	125 mL
Ricotta cheese	1/4 cup	60 mL
Chopped fresh parsley	1/4 cup	60 mL
Chopped fresh sage (or 3/4 tsp., 4 mL, dried)	1 tbsp.	15 mL
Salt	1/4 tsp.	1 mL
Orange marmalade	3 tbsp.	50 mL
Maple (or maple-flavoured) syrup	2 tbsp.	30 mL
Coarse ground pepper	1/4 tsp.	1 mL

Cut tenderloin almost in half lengthwise, not quite through to other side. Press open to flatten. Place between 2 pieces of plastic wrap. Pound with mallet or rolling pin to even 1/2 inch (12 mm) thickness. Remove and discard plastic wrap.

Spread mustard evenly over tenderloin to edges. Arrange red pepper over mustard, leaving 1 inch (2.5 cm) edge all around.

Combine next 4 ingredients in small bowl. Carefully spread over red pepper. Roll up, jelly roll-style, from long side to enclose filling. Tie with butcher's string or secure with metal skewers. Place, seam-side up, on greased wire rack set in small roasting pan.

Measure marmalade, syrup and pepper into small cup. Stir. Brush about 1/2 of mixture evenly over tenderloin. Cover. Cook in 350°F (175°C) oven for 20 minutes. Remove from oven. Lightly brush tenderloin with 1/2 of remaining marmalade mixture. Turn tenderloin over. Lightly brush with remaining marmalade mixture. Cook for 20 to 25 minutes until meat thermometer inserted into thickest part of tenderloin (not stuffing) reads 155°F (68°C), or until desired doneness. Remove from oven. Cover with foil. Let stand for 10 minutes. Internal temperature should rise to at least 160°F (70°C). Remove butcher's string. Cut on diagonal into 1/2 inch (12 mm) thick slices. Serves 4.

1 serving: 323 Calories; 15.9 g Total Fat (6.6 g Mono, 1.8 g Poly, 6 g Sat); 75 mg Cholesterol; 19 g Carbohydrate; trace Fibre; 26 g Protein; 328 mg Sodium

Pepper Sage Pork

Lovely herbed roast. Serve with Rosemary Sautéed Potatoes, page 109, and Braised Red Cabbage, page 110.

Unsweetened applesauce	1/4 cup	60 mL
Apple juice	2 tbsp.	30 mL
Brown sugar, packed	2 tbsp.	30 mL
Chopped fresh sage (or 1 1/2 tsp., 7 mL, dried)	2 tbsp.	30 mL
Dijon mustard (with whole seeds)	2 tbsp.	30 mL
Coarse ground pepper	2 tsp.	10 mL
Dried savory (optional)	1 tsp.	5 mL
Lean boneless pork loin roast	2 1/2 lbs.	1.1 kg

Measure first 7 ingredients into small bowl. Stir well.

Place pork loin on greased wire rack set in small roasting pan. Spread 1/2 of applesauce mixture evenly over top. Cover. Cook in 450°F (230°C) oven for 15 minutes. Reduce heat to 350°F (175°C). Cook for about 1 1/2 hours, brushing several times with remaining applesauce mixture, until meat thermometer inserted into thickest part of pork loin reads 155°F (68°C), or until desired doneness. Remove from oven. Cover with foil. Let stand for 10 minutes. Internal temperature should rise to at least 160°F (70°C). Cut into 1/4 inch (6 mm) thick slices. Serves 10.

1 serving: 154 Calories; 6 g Total Fat (2.6 g Mono, 0.8 g Poly, 2 g Sat); 49 mg Cholesterol; 4 g Carbohydrate; trace Fibre; 20 g Protein; 83 mg Sodium

Paré Pointer

She refused to work at the toll booth because her mom and dad always said not to take money from strangers.

Garlic Rosemary Lamb

Garlic and rosemary herb coating sweetened with a touch of honey.

Chopped fresh parsley	1/4 cup	60 mL
Olive (or cooking) oil	2 tbsp.	30 mL
Garlic cloves, minced	6	6
Liquid honey	1 tbsp.	15 mL
Finely chopped fresh rosemary leaves (or 3/4 tsp., 4 mL, dried)	1 tbsp.	15 mL
Finely grated lemon zest	2 tsp.	10 mL
Dried crushed chilies	1/4 – 1/2 tsp.	1 – 2 mL
Salt	1/2 tsp.	2 mL
Rack of lamb (4 to 6 ribs)	12 oz.	340 g

Combine first 8 ingredients in small bowl.

Cover tips of bones of lamb rack with foil, if desired, to prevent darkening during cooking. Press parsley mixture onto each side of lamb rack. Let stand for 20 minutes. Preheat small roasting pan in 475°F (240°C) oven for 5 minutes. Place lamb, bone-side down, on greased wire rack set in same roasting pan. Cook, uncovered, for 10 minutes. Reduce heat to 375°F (190°C). Cover. Cook for about 20 minutes until meat thermometer inserted into thickest part of lamb rack reads 155°F (68°C), or until desired doneness. Remove from oven. Cover with foil. Let stand for 10 minutes. Internal temperature should rise to at least 160°F (70°C). Cut between ribs to serve. Serves 2.

1 serving: 517 Calories; 42.4 g Total Fat (22.1 g Mono, 3.3 g Poly, 14.1 g Sat); 93 mg Cholesterol; 13 g Carbohydrate; trace Fibre; 21 g Protein; 673 mg Sodium

Pictured on front cover.

 To crush peppercorns, place whole peppercorns in a small plastic bag. Tap peppercorns with a heavy object, such as a mallet or hammer, until coarsely crushed.

Lamb Hot Pot

Somewhat spicy, curry-like sauce with tender lamb and sweet carrots.
Serve with rice and a dollop of yogurt to tame the spice.

Medium onions, quartered	3	3
Garlic cloves	3	3
Finely grated, peeled gingerroot	2 tsp.	10 mL
Ground coriander	2 tsp.	10 mL
Salt	1 1/2 tsp.	7 mL
Ground cumin	1 tsp.	5 mL
Turmeric	1 tsp.	5 mL
Dried crushed chilies	1/4 tsp.	1 mL
Lean boneless lamb, cut into 1 inch (2.5 cm) cubes (or lamb stew meat)	2 lbs.	900 g
Cooking oil	1 tbsp.	15 mL
Diced carrot	2 cups	500 mL
Water	1 cup	250 mL

Process first 8 ingredients in blender or food processor, scraping down sides if necessary, until onion is finely chopped. Transfer to medium bowl.

Add lamb. Stir until coated. Let stand for 30 minutes to marinate.

Heat cooking oil in large frying pan on medium. Cook lamb mixture in hot cooking oil until lamb is browned on all sides.

Add carrot and water. Stir. Reduce heat to medium-low. Cover. Simmer for about 60 minutes, stirring occasionally, until lamb is tender and carrot is softened. Makes 4 cups (1 L). Serves 8.

1 serving: 197 Calories; 8 g Total Fat (3.5 g Mono, 1.1 g Poly, 2.3 g Sat); 73 mg Cholesterol; 7 g Carbohydrate; 1 g Fibre; 24 g Protein; 535 mg Sodium

Paré Pointer

She didn't get her shoes repaired because
she didn't want to add insole to injury.

Herb-Crusted Lamb Rack

Mint, lemon and rosemary complement lamb in this elegant dish.
Tender and flavourful.

Fresh white bread slice (with crusts)	1/2	1/2
Grated Parmesan cheese	1/3 cup	75 mL
Chopped fresh mint leaves	3 tbsp.	50 mL
Sesame seeds, toasted (see Tip, page 33)	2 tbsp.	30 mL
Chopped fresh rosemary leaves	2 tsp.	10 mL
Finely grated lemon zest	1 tsp.	5 mL
Garlic clove, minced (or 1/4 tsp., 1 mL, powder)	1	1
Salt	1/4 tsp.	1 mL
Pepper	1/2 tsp.	2 mL
Hard margarine (or butter), melted	2 tbsp.	30 mL
Rack of lamb (about 8 ribs), bones frenched (see Note)	1 1/4 lbs.	560 g

Process bread in blender or food processor until coarse crumbs.

Add next 8 ingredients. Pulse with on/off motion until just combined. Transfer to medium bowl.

Drizzle with melted margarine. Toss lightly until just moistened.

Cover tips of bones of lamb rack with foil, if desired, to prevent darkening during cooking. Press bread mixture onto meaty side of lamb rack, bone-side up. Place on greased wire rack set in small roasting pan. Cook, uncovered, in 425°F (220°C) oven for 10 minutes. Cover. Reduce heat to 375°F (190°C). Cook for about 25 minutes until meat thermometer inserted into thickest part of lamb rack reads 155°F (68°C), or until desired doneness. Remove from oven. Cover with foil. Let stand for 10 minutes. Internal temperature should rise to at least 160°F (70°C). Cut between ribs to serve. Serves 4.

1 serving: 413 Calories; 34.3 g Total Fat (15.3 g Mono, 3.4 g Poly, 13.3 g Sat); 83 mg Cholesterol; 4 g Carbohydrate; 1 g Fibre; 22 g Protein; 456 mg Sodium

Note: To french bones, cut meat away from end of rib so that part of bone is exposed, creating a fancier presentation.

Entrées

Aniseed Tofu

The spices make this an appealing dish. Serve over brown rice.

Cooking oil	2 tsp.	10 mL
Thinly sliced green onion	1/4 cup	60 mL
Finely grated, peeled gingerroot	1 tsp.	5 mL
Garlic cloves, minced (or 1/2 tsp., 2 mL, powder)	2	2
Dried crushed chilies	1/2 tsp.	2 mL
Pepper	1/4 tsp.	1 mL
Water	3/4 cup	175 mL
Soy sauce	2 tbsp.	30 mL
Liquid honey	2 tbsp.	30 mL
Dry sherry	2 tbsp.	30 mL
Star anise	1	1
Package of extra-firm tofu, drained and cut into 3/4 inch (2 cm) cubes	12 1/2 oz.	350 g
Water	1 tbsp.	15 mL
Cornstarch	1 1/2 tsp.	7 mL
Thinly sliced green onion, for garnish	2 tsp.	10 mL
Sesame seeds, toasted (see Tip, page 33), for garnish	1/2 tsp.	2 mL

Heat wok or medium frying pan on medium until hot. Add cooking oil. Add next 5 ingredients. Stir-fry for about 3 minutes until onion is softened.

Add next 5 ingredients. Stir. Bring to a boil. Reduce heat to medium-low. Cover. Simmer for 10 minutes, stirring occasionally. Transfer to small bowl. Let stand for 5 minutes.

Add tofu. Stir gently until coated. Cover. Marinate in refrigerator for at least 8 hours or overnight, stirring occasionally. Remove tofu to separate small bowl using slotted spoon. Set aside. Pour marinade into wok or medium frying pan. Bring to a boil on medium-high.

Stir second amount of water into cornstarch in small cup until smooth. Slowly add to marinade, stirring constantly. Heat and stir until boiling and thickened. Remove and discard star anise. Add tofu. Cook for 2 to 3 minutes until heated through. Transfer to serving dish.

Sprinkle with second amount of green onion and sesame seeds. Makes about 2 1/2 cups (625 mL). Serves 4.

1 serving: 201 Calories; 10 g Total Fat (3.1 g Mono, 5 g Poly, 1.3 g Sat); 0 mg Cholesterol; 16 g Carbohydrate; 1 g Fibre; 15 g Protein; 540 mg Sodium

Megadarra

(Mah-ZJAHD-ruh) originates in Lebanon. The sweetness of the onions and the earthiness of the lentils are a delicious combination. A great meatless meal. Serve with a crisp green salad.

Olive (or cooking) oil	1 tbsp.	15 mL
Thinly sliced onion	3 1/2 cups	875 mL
Brown sugar, packed	2 tbsp.	30 mL
Red wine vinegar	1 tbsp.	15 mL
Dried green lentils	1 cup	250 mL
Cans of condensed vegetable broth (10 oz., 284 mL, each)	2	2
Water	1/2 cup	125 mL
Coarse ground pepper	1/2 tsp.	2 mL
Ground allspice	1/2 tsp.	2 mL
Ground coriander	1/2 tsp.	2 mL
Brown converted rice	1/2 cup	125 mL
Can of condensed vegetable broth	10 oz.	284 mL
Water	3/4 cup	175 mL
Chopped fresh parsley (or 1 1/2 tsp., 7 mL, flakes)	2 tbsp.	30 mL

Heat olive oil in large frying pan on medium. Add onion. Cook for about 20 minutes, stirring often, until caramelized.

Add brown sugar and vinegar. Heat and stir for 1 minute. Remove from heat. Set aside.

Measure next 6 ingredients into large saucepan. Stir. Bring to a boil on medium. Reduce heat to medium-low. Cover. Simmer for about 20 minutes, without stirring, until lentils are almost tender.

Add rice, second amount of broth, water and 1/2 of onion mixture. Stir. Bring to a boil on medium. Reduce heat to medium-low. Cover. Simmer for 20 to 25 minutes, without stirring, until rice is tender. Transfer to serving dish.

Top with remaining onion mixture and parsley. Makes 5 cups (1.25 L).

1 cup (250 mL): 358 Calories; 5.8 g Total Fat (3.2 g Mono, 1.1 g Poly, 1.1 g Sat); 2 mg Cholesterol; 56 g Carbohydrate; 7 g Fibre; 22 g Protein; 1144 mg Sodium

Pictured on page 125.

Basil Lentil Burgers

A flavourful, low-fat alternative to beef burgers. Just add condiments.

Boiling water	1/4 cup	60 mL
Bulgur	1/4 cup	60 mL
Red lentils	3 tbsp.	50 mL
Water	1/2 cup	125 mL
Can of navy beans, drained and rinsed	14 oz.	398 mL
Hard margarine (or butter)	1 1/2 tbsp.	25 mL
Chopped onion	1 1/4 cups	300 mL
Garlic clove, minced (or 1/4 tsp., 1 mL, powder)	1	1
Fine dry bread crumbs	1/2 cup	125 mL
Chopped fresh basil	1/4 cup	60 mL
Chopped fresh parsley	1 tbsp.	15 mL
Large egg, fork-beaten	1	1
Salt	1/2 tsp.	2 mL
Pepper	1/4 tsp.	1 mL
Cooking oil	2 tbsp.	30 mL
Hamburger buns, split and buttered	8	8

Pour boiling water over bulgur in small bowl. Cover. Let stand for 15 minutes.

Measure lentils and second amount of water into small saucepan. Bring to a boil on medium. Reduce heat to low. Cover. Simmer for about 20 minutes, without stirring, until lentils are tender and liquid is evaporated.

Place navy beans in blender or food processor. Add lentils. Process until coarsely ground.

Melt margarine in small frying pan on medium. Add onion. Cook for 5 to 10 minutes, stirring often, until softened. Add garlic. Heat and stir for 1 to 2 minutes until fragrant. Transfer to large bowl. Let stand for 5 minutes.

Add next 6 ingredients. Add lentil mixture and bulgur. Stir well. Shape mixture into 8 patties, using about 1/4 cup (60 mL) for each.

Heat cooking oil in large frying pan on medium. Place patties in pan. Cook for about 3 minutes per side until golden.

Place 1 patty on bottom half of each bun. Cover with top halves of buns. Makes 8 burgers.

1 burger: 294 Calories; 9.2 g Total Fat (5 g Mono, 2 g Poly, 1.6 g Sat); 27 mg Cholesterol; 43 g Carbohydrate; 4 g Fibre; 10 g Protein; 555 mg Sodium

Creamy Spinach Lasagne

Cheesy and creamy pasta dish with a robust herb and spinach layer. Satisfying herb flavour.

Lasagna noodles, each broken into 3 equal pieces	6	6
Boiling water	8 cups	2 L
Salt	1 tsp.	5 mL
WHITE SAUCE		
Hard margarine (or butter)	3 tbsp.	50 mL
All-purpose flour	3 tbsp.	50 mL
Homogenized milk	3 cups	750 mL
Garlic salt	1 1/2 tsp.	7 mL
Onion powder	1/4 tsp.	1 mL
Pepper, sprinkle		
Box of frozen chopped spinach, thawed and squeezed dry	10 oz.	300 g
Ricotta cheese	9 oz.	250 g
Grated part-skim mozzarella cheese	1 cup	250 mL
Grated Parmesan cheese	2 tbsp.	30 mL
Chopped fresh basil (or 1 1/2 tsp., 7 mL, dried)	2 tbsp.	30 mL
Chopped fresh marjoram leaves (or 3/4 tsp., 4 mL, dried)	1 tbsp.	15 mL
Chopped fresh rosemary leaves (or 1/4 tsp., 1 mL, ground)	1 tsp.	5 mL
Green onion, sliced	1	1
Egg yolk (large)	1	1
Grated part-skim mozzarella cheese	3/4 cup	175 mL
Grated Parmesan cheese	1 tbsp.	15 mL

Cook noodles in boiling water and salt in large uncovered pot or Dutch oven for 12 to 15 minutes, stirring occasionally, until tender but firm. Drain. Rinse with cold water. Set aside.

(continued on next page)

White Sauce: Melt margarine in medium saucepan on medium. Add flour. Heat and stir for about 1 minute until smooth.

Slowly add milk, stirring constantly, until combined. Heat and stir for about 10 minutes until boiling and thickened. Remove from heat.

Add garlic salt, onion powder and pepper. Stir. Makes 2 3/4 cups (675 mL) sauce. Spoon about 1/2 cup (125 mL) sauce into greased 2 quart (2 L) shallow baking dish. Spread evenly. Layer 1/2 of noodles evenly over sauce.

Combine next 9 ingredients in medium bowl. Add 1 cup (250 mL) sauce. Stir. Spread evenly over noodles. Cover with remaining noodles. Pour remaining sauce over top. Spread evenly. Cover with greased foil. Bake in 350°F (175°C) oven for about 45 minutes until heated through. Remove foil.

Sprinkle second amounts of mozzarella cheese and Parmesan cheese over top. Bake, uncovered, for about 30 minutes until cheese is golden. Let stand on wire rack for 15 minutes before serving. Serves 6.

1 serving: *417 Calories; 23.5 g Total Fat (8.8 g Mono, 1.4 g Poly, 11.9 g Sat); 98 mg Cholesterol; 28 g Carbohydrate; 2 g Fibre; 23 g Protein; 713 mg Sodium*

Pictured on page 125.

Paré Pointer

Susan has a big collection of books. The trouble is no one ever lends shelves.

Vegetarian Pesto Lasagne

Lots of ingredients and several steps in the preparation, but a wonderful result. Colourful layers with smooth, creamy pesto sauce.

PARSLEY BASIL PESTO

Pecan pieces, toasted (see Tip, page 33)	1/2 cup	125 mL
Fresh basil leaves, packed	1/2 cup	125 mL
Fresh parsley sprigs, packed	1/2 cup	125 mL
Olive (or cooking) oil	1/3 cup	75 mL
Grated Parmesan cheese	3 tbsp.	50 mL
Garlic cloves, quartered	2	2
Salt	1/4 tsp.	1 mL
Pepper	1/4 tsp.	1 mL

CHEESE SAUCE

Hard margarine (or butter)	1/4 cup	60 mL
All-purpose flour	1/4 cup	60 mL
Milk	2 1/4 cups	550 mL
Grated part-skim mozzarella cheese	1/3 cup	75 mL
Grated Parmesan cheese	1/4 cup	60 mL
Ground nutmeg	1/2 tsp.	2 mL
Pepper, just a pinch		
Medium eggplants, cut lengthwise into 1/3 inch (1 cm) thick slices (about 18 slices, total)	3	3
Salt	2 tsp.	10 mL
Olive (or cooking) oil	2 1/2 tbsp.	37 mL
Jar of spaghetti sauce	25 oz.	700 mL
Oven-ready lasagna noodles	9	9
Jars of roasted red peppers (13 oz., 370 mL, each), drained and cut into 1/2 inch (12 mm) thick strips	2	2

Parsley Basil Pesto: Process all 8 ingredients in blender or food processor until smooth. Set aside. Makes 3/4 cup (175 mL) pesto.

(continued on next page)

Entrées

Cheese Sauce: Melt margarine in medium saucepan on medium. Add flour. Heat and stir for about 1 minute until smooth.

Slowly add milk, stirring constantly, until combined. Heat and stir for about 10 minutes until boiling and thickened. Remove from heat.

Add next 4 ingredients. Stir until cheese is melted. Set aside. Makes 2 1/4 cups (550 mL) cheese sauce.

Place eggplant slices on wire racks set in baking sheets with sides. Sprinkle with salt. Let stand for 15 minutes. Rinse under running water. Pat dry with paper towels.

Brush both sides of each eggplant slice with olive oil. Arrange in single layer on ungreased baking sheets. Bake in 375°F (190°C) oven for 50 to 55 minutes until softened, turning slices once and changing position of baking sheets halfway through baking time. Remove from oven. Divide and spread pesto on 1 side of each eggplant slice.

Layer ingredients in greased 9 x 13 inch (22 x 33 cm) pan as follows:

1. 1 cup (250 mL) spaghetti sauce, spread evenly in pan
2. 3 lasagna noodles
3. 1/2 of eggplant slices
4. 1/2 of red pepper strips
5. 1 cup (250 mL) spaghetti sauce
6. 3 lasagna noodles
7. Remaining eggplant slices
8. Remaining red pepper strips
9. Remaining spaghetti sauce
10. Remaining 3 lasagna noodles
11. Cheese Sauce, spread evenly over top

Cover with greased foil. Bake in 350°F (175°C) oven for about 60 minutes until bubbling and noodles are softened. Remove foil. Broil on middle rack in oven for 10 to 15 minutes until golden. Let stand for about 10 minutes until set. Serves 8.

1 serving: 547 Calories; 33.6 g Total Fat (20.7 g Mono, 4.7 g Poly, 6.4 g Sat); 10 mg Cholesterol; 52 g Carbohydrate; 3 g Fibre; 14 g Protein; 1481 mg Sodium

Glazed Roasted Carrots

Lightly glazed and slightly sweet. Thyme goes well with carrots.

Large carrots, peeled (about 2 lbs., 900 g)	7	7
Olive (or cooking) oil	2 tsp.	10 mL
Garlic powder	1/2 tsp.	2 mL
Ground cumin	1/4 tsp.	1 mL
Salt	1/4 tsp.	1 mL
Pepper	1/4 tsp.	1 mL
Maple (or maple-flavoured) syrup	3 tbsp.	50 mL
Chopped fresh thyme leaves (or 1/2 tsp., 2 mL, dried)	2 tsp.	10 mL

Cut carrots in half crosswise. Cut each piece lengthwise into quarters. Place in large bowl.

Add next 5 ingredients. Toss until coated. Spread in single layer on ungreased baking sheet. Bake in 375°F (190°C) oven for about 30 minutes, stirring occasionally, until carrots are tender.

Drizzle with maple syrup. Sprinkle with thyme. Carefully stir carrots until coated. Bake for about 10 minutes until glazed. Serves 4.

1 serving: 159 Calories; 2.8 g Total Fat (1.7 g Mono, 0.4 g Poly, 0.4 g Sat); 0 mg Cholesterol; 33 g Carbohydrate; 6 g Fibre; 2 g Protein; 229 mg Sodium

Pictured on page 126.

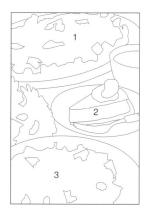

1. Sirloin Strips, page 80
2. Nutmeg Cheesecake, page 148
3. Cranberry Salad, page 58

Side Dishes

Rosemary Sautéed Potatoes

Peel the potatoes if you prefer. They'll be just as good!

Large baking potatoes (with skin), about 2 1/2 lbs. (1.1 kg)	4	4
Water		
Olive (or cooking) oil	1/4 cup	60 mL
Garlic clove, minced (or 1/4 tsp., 1 mL, powder)	1	1
Chopped fresh rosemary leaves (or 3/4 tsp., 4 mL, dried)	1 tbsp.	15 mL
Jean's Jazz, page 14 (or Seasoned Salt, page 14)	2 tsp.	10 mL

Cook whole potatoes in water in large saucepan until just tender. Drain. Cool. Cut into 1 inch (2.5 cm) cubes.

Heat olive oil in large frying pan on medium. Add potatoes, garlic and rosemary. Cook for about 1 minute, stirring gently, until potatoes are coated.

Add Jean's Jazz. Cook, stirring occasionally, until potatoes are heated through and browned. Serves 6.

1 serving: 227 Calories; 9.9 g Total Fat (7.1 g Mono, 0.9 g Poly, 1.4 g Sat); 0 mg Cholesterol; 32 g Carbohydrate; 3 g Fibre; 4 g Protein; 277 mg Sodium

Pictured on page 126.

1. Mussels And Pasta Shells, page 86
2. Coconut Fish Curry, page 85
3. Cajun Garlic Shrimp, page 91

Props Courtesy Of: Danesco Inc.

Braised Red Cabbage

Tangy and flavourful. Serve with Pepper Sage Pork, page 95, or Garlic Rosemary Lamb, page 96.

Cooking oil	2 tbsp.	30 mL
Chopped onion	1 cup	250 mL
Garlic cloves, minced (or 1/2 tsp., 2 mL, powder)	2	2
Shredded red cabbage (2 – 2 1/2 lbs., 900 g – 1.1 kg)	9 cups	2.25 L
Tart medium cooking apples (such as Granny Smith), peeled and cored, chopped	3	3
Can of condensed chicken broth	10 oz.	284 mL
Red wine vinegar	1/2 cup	125 mL
Granulated sugar	1/4 cup	60 mL
Caraway seed	1 tbsp.	15 mL
Bay leaves	3	3
Salt	1/2 tsp.	2 mL
Pepper	1/2 tsp.	2 mL

Heat cooking oil in large pot or Dutch oven on medium. Add onion and garlic. Cook for about 1 minute, stirring often, until fragrant.

Add next 7 ingredients. Stir well. Bring to a boil. Reduce heat to medium-low. Cover. Simmer for about 45 minutes, stirring occasionally, until cabbage is softened. Remove and discard bay leaves.

Add salt and pepper. Stir. Makes 7 1/2 cups (1.9 L).

1/2 cup (125 mL): 75 Calories; 2.4 g Total Fat (1.2 g Mono, 0.7 g Poly, 0.2 g Sat); 0 mg Cholesterol; 13 g Carbohydrate; 2 g Fibre; 2 g Protein; 212 mg Sodium

Pictured on page 126.

Paré Pointer
Even if you march to the beat of a different drummer, bring the speed up.

Side Dishes

Pistachio And Apricot Pilaf

Exotic spices mingled with delicately sweet apricots. Saffron costs a bit more than most spices, but it makes a delicious difference.

Cooking oil	1 tbsp.	15 mL
Chopped onion	2 cups	500 mL
Finely grated, peeled gingerroot	1 tsp.	5 mL
Ground coriander	1 tsp.	5 mL
Garlic cloves, minced (or 1/2 tsp., 2 mL, powder)	2	2
Cinnamon stick (4 inches, 10 cm)	1	1
Green chili, seeds and ribs removed (see Tip, page 135), finely chopped	1	1
Crushed saffron threads (or turmeric)	1/8 tsp.	0.5 mL
Prepared chicken (or vegetable) broth	2 cups	500 mL
Basmati (or long grain) white rice	1 cup	250 mL
Coarsely grated carrot	1/2 cup	125 mL
Salt	1/2 tsp.	2 mL
Coarsely chopped pistachios, toasted (see Tip, page 33)	1/3 cup	75 mL
Finely chopped dried apricots	1/3 cup	75 mL

Heat cooking oil in large saucepan on medium. Add onion. Cook for 5 to 10 minutes, stirring often, until softened.

Add next 6 ingredients. Heat and stir for 1 to 2 minutes until fragrant.

Add next 4 ingredients. Stir. Bring to a boil. Reduce heat to medium-low. Cover. Simmer for 15 minutes, without stirring. Remove from heat.

Add pistachios and apricots. Stir. Cover. Let stand for 10 minutes. Remove cinnamon stick. Fluff rice with fork. Makes 5 1/2 cups (1.4 L). Serves 6.

1 serving: 248 Calories; 7.2 g Total Fat (4.4 g Mono, 1.5 g Poly, 0.9 g Sat); 0 mg Cholesterol; 40 g Carbohydrate; 3 g Fibre; 6 g Protein; 480 mg Sodium

Pictured on front cover.

Curry Fried Rice

Vibrant yellow curry gives this dish a distinct Thai flavour.

Long grain white rice	1 cup	250 mL
Medium sweetened coconut, toasted (see Tip, page 33)	1/3 cup	75 mL
Water	2 cups	500 mL
Salt	1/2 tsp.	2 mL
Cooking oil	1 tbsp.	15 mL
Boneless, skinless chicken breast halves (about 2), chopped	8 oz.	225 g
Salt	1/2 tsp.	2 mL
Pepper	1/4 tsp.	1 mL
Cayenne pepper	1/16 tsp.	0.5 mL
Finely chopped red pepper	1 cup	250 mL
Finely chopped red onion	2/3 cup	150 mL
Finely grated, peeled gingerroot	1 tsp.	5 mL
Curry powder	4 tsp.	20 mL
Cooking oil	1 tbsp.	15 mL
Large eggs, fork-beaten	2	2
Can of baby corn, drained and chopped	14 oz.	398 mL
Chopped fresh cilantro or parsley (or 1 1/2 tsp., 7 mL, dried)	2 tbsp.	30 mL
Green onions, sliced thinly	2	2

Measure first 4 ingredients into medium saucepan. Bring to a boil on medium. Reduce heat to medium-low. Cover. Simmer for 15 minutes, without stirring. Remove from heat. Let stand, covered, for about 5 minutes until rice is tender. Fluff with fork. Cool.

Heat wok or large frying pan on medium-high until very hot. Add first amount of cooking oil. Add chicken. Sprinkle with salt, pepper and cayenne pepper. Stir-fry for 4 to 5 minutes until chicken is no longer pink.

Add red pepper, onion and ginger. Stir-fry for 3 to 4 minutes until onion is softened.

(continued on next page)

112 Side Dishes

Add curry powder. Stir-fry for about 1 minute until fragrant. Transfer to medium bowl. Cover to keep warm.

Heat second amount of cooking oil in wok. Add egg. Cook for about 1 minute, without stirring, until almost firm. Turn. Immediately cut egg with edge of lifter until finely chopped.

Add rice mixture and corn. Stir-fry, breaking up rice, until corn is hot. Add chicken mixture. Stir-fry for about 1 minute until heated through. Transfer to serving platter.

Sprinkle with cilantro and green onion. Makes 7 cups (1.75 L).

1 cup (250 mL): 259 Calories; 7.7 g Total Fat (3.2 g Mono, 1.7 g Poly, 2 g Sat); 80 mg Cholesterol; 35 g Carbohydrate; 2 g Fibre; 13 g Protein; 474 mg Sodium

Pictured on page 90.

Chili Lime Beans

Lime-flavoured, spicy green beans coated with a light, creamy sauce.

Fresh (or frozen) whole green beans	1 lb.	454 g
Water		
Salt, just a pinch		
Hard margarine (or butter)	1/4 cup	60 mL
Sour cream	2 tbsp.	30 mL
Lime juice	2 tbsp.	30 mL
Dried crushed chilies	1/2 – 1 tsp.	2 – 5 mL
Caraway seed, toasted (see Note)	2 tsp.	10 mL

Cook beans in water and salt in medium saucepan until tender-crisp. Drain. Transfer to large bowl. Cover to keep warm.

Melt margarine in same saucepan on medium. Add sour cream, lime juice and chilies. Heat and stir for about 1 minute until hot. Add to beans. Toss until coated.

Sprinkle with caraway seed. Makes 3 cups (750 mL). Serves 4.

1 serving: 162 Calories; 13.5 g Total Fat (8.3 g Mono, 1.3 g Poly, 3.2 g Sat); 3 mg Cholesterol; 10 g Carbohydrate; 2 g Fibre; 3 g Protein; 156 mg Sodium

Note: Toast caraway seed in small ungreased frying pan on medium until they make a snapping sound.

Zucchini Bacon Risotto

Smoky bacon and creamy Parmesan cheese with tender arborio (ar-BOHR-ee-oh) rice. It's a delicious way to use parsley that we often have an abundance of in the refrigerator, window pot or garden.

Small zucchini, cut lengthwise into 1/4 inch (6 mm) thick slices	2	2
Chili sauce	2 tbsp.	30 mL
Bacon slices, diced	6	6
Olive (or cooking) oil	1 tbsp.	15 mL
Hard margarine (or butter)	1 tbsp.	15 mL
Finely chopped onion	1 cup	250 mL
Prepared chicken broth	6 cups	1.5 L
Arborio (or short grain white) rice	2 cups	500 mL
Dry white (or alcohol-free) wine	1/2 cup	125 mL
Sour cream	3 tbsp.	50 mL
Grated Parmesan cheese	1/3 cup	75 mL
Chopped fresh parsley	1/4 cup	60 mL
Finely grated lemon zest	1/2 tsp.	2 mL
Pepper, just a pinch		

Spray zucchini with cooking spray. Divide and brush chili sauce on both sides of each zucchini slice. Preheat electric grill for 5 minutes or gas barbecue to medium. Cook zucchini on greased grill (or broil in oven) for 3 to 4 minutes per side until tender and grill marks appear. Cut crosswise into 1 inch (2.5 cm) pieces. Transfer to small bowl. Set aside.

Cook bacon in large saucepan on medium until almost crisp. Remove to paper towels to drain. Remove and discard drippings.

Heat olive oil and margarine in same large saucepan on medium. Add onion. Cook for 5 to 10 minutes, stirring often, until softened.

Measure chicken broth into medium saucepan. Cover. Bring to a boil on medium. Reduce heat to low. Cover.

(continued on next page)

Add rice to onion mixture. Stir until coated. Add wine. Heat and stir until wine is absorbed. Add 1 cup (250 mL) hot broth, stirring constantly, until broth is absorbed. Repeat with remaining broth, 1 cup (250 mL) at a time, until all broth is absorbed and rice is tender. Entire process will take about 25 minutes.

Add sour cream, stirring constantly, until hot. Remove from heat. Add remaining 4 ingredients. Add reserved zucchini and bacon. Stir well. Makes 8 cups (2 L).

1 cup (250 mL): 333 Calories; 9.1 g Total Fat (4.5 g Mono, 0.9 g Poly, 3.1 g Sat); 10 mg Cholesterol; 47 g Carbohydrate; 1 g Fibre; 12 g Protein; 854 mg Sodium

Orange Spiced Lentils

A complementary side dish for Spiced Butter Chicken, page 70, or Stuffed Pork Loin, page 93.

Green lentils	1 cup	250 mL
Water		
Cooking oil	2 tsp.	10 mL
Finely chopped onion	1/2 cup	125 mL
Ground cumin	1/2 tsp.	2 mL
Ground cinnamon	1/2 tsp.	2 mL
Orange juice	1 cup	250 mL
Water	1 cup	250 mL
Whole cloves	3	3
Chopped fresh parsley (or 1 1/2 tsp., 7 mL, flakes)	2 tbsp.	30 mL
Salt	1/2 tsp.	2 mL

Cover lentils with water in large bowl. Let stand overnight. Drain.

Heat cooking oil in medium saucepan on medium. Add onion. Cook for 5 to 10 minutes, stirring often, until softened. Add cumin and cinnamon. Heat and stir for about 1 minute until fragrant.

Add lentils and next 3 ingredients. Stir. Bring to a boil. Reduce heat to medium-low. Simmer, uncovered, for about 70 minutes, without stirring, until liquid is absorbed and lentils are softened.

Add parsley and salt. Stir well. Remove and discard cloves. Makes 2 1/2 cups (625 mL). Serves 4.

1 serving: 232 Calories; 3 g Total Fat (1.5 g Mono, 1 g Poly, 0.3 g Sat); 0 mg Cholesterol; 38 g Carbohydrate; 6 g Fibre; 15 g Protein; 305 mg Sodium

Feta Herb Ravioli

Tomato sauce, feta cheese and fresh herbs create a flavour sensation.

TOMATO SAUCE		
Olive (or cooking) oil	1/2 tbsp.	7 mL
Chopped red onion	1/2 cup	125 mL
Garlic clove, minced (or 1/4 tsp., 1 mL, powder)	1	1
Can of diced tomatoes (with juice)	14 oz.	398 mL
Balsamic vinegar	1/2 tsp.	2 mL
Granulated sugar	1/2 tsp.	2 mL
Salt, sprinkle		
Crumbled feta cheese (about 4 oz., 113 g)	3/4 cup	175 mL
Chopped fresh basil	2 tbsp.	30 mL
Chopped fresh parsley	2 tbsp.	30 mL
Large egg, fork-beaten	1	1
Ground nutmeg	1/4 tsp.	1 mL
Pepper	1/4 tsp.	1 mL
Wonton wrappers	32	32
Large egg, fork-beaten	1	1
Boiling water		

Tomato Sauce: Heat olive oil in large frying pan on medium. Add onion. Cook for 5 to 10 minutes, stirring often, until softened. Add garlic. Heat and stir for 1 to 2 minutes until fragrant.

Add next 4 ingredients. Stir. Bring to a boil. Boil for about 5 minutes, stirring occasionally, until thickened. Remove from heat. Cover to keep warm. Makes 1 1/3 cups (325 mL) sauce.

Measure next 6 ingredients into medium bowl. Stir.

Place 2 tsp. (10 mL) feta cheese mixture in centre of 1 wonton wrapper. Brush edges with some of second amount of egg. Place second wonton wrapper on top. Press edges to seal. Place on waxed paper-lined baking sheet. Cover ravioli with tea towel to prevent drying. Repeat with remaining feta cheese mixture, wonton wrappers and egg. Makes 16 ravioli.

Cook ravioli in boiling water in large uncovered pot or Dutch oven for about 3 minutes, stirring occasionally, until wrappers are tender but firm. Drain well. Place 4 ravioli on each of 4 individual plates. Divide and spoon sauce over ravioli. Serves 4.

1 serving: 349 Calories; 11.8 g Total Fat (3.7 g Mono, 1.2 g Poly, 5.6 g Sat); 140 mg Cholesterol; 46 g Carbohydrate; 1 g Fibre; 15 g Protein; 890 mg Sodium

Squash And Sage Pasta

Earthy flavours complement the sweet, nutty taste of roasted squash.

Chopped butternut squash	4 cups	1 L
Cooking oil	2 tsp.	10 mL
Chopped fresh sage	2 tsp.	10 mL
Salt	1/4 tsp.	1 mL
Pepper	1/4 tsp.	1 mL
Cooking oil	3 tbsp.	50 mL
Fresh sage leaves	12	12
Sliced fresh brown (or white) mushrooms	2 1/2 cups	625 mL
Garlic cloves, minced	2	2
Prepared chicken (or vegetable) broth	1 cup	250 mL
Bow pasta (about 5 oz., 140 g)	2 cups	500 mL
Boiling water	8 cups	2 L
Salt	1 tsp.	5 mL
Grated Parmesan cheese	1/3 cup	75 mL
Pine nuts, toasted (see Tip, page 33)	1/4 cup	60 mL

Measure first 5 ingredients into large bowl. Toss until squash is coated. Spread in single layer on greased baking sheet. Bake in 375°F (190°C) oven for about 40 minutes, turning occasionally, until lightly browned but not mushy. Remove to same large bowl. Cover to keep warm.

Heat second amount of cooking oil in large frying pan on medium. Add sage leaves. Heat and stir for about 1 minute until crisp. Remove to paper towels to drain, using tongs or slotted spoon. Set aside. Reserve cooking oil in pan.

Heat reserved cooking oil on medium-high. Add mushrooms. Cook for about 5 minutes, stirring occasionally, until lightly browned.

Add garlic. Heat and stir for 1 to 2 minutes until fragrant. Add broth. Stir. Bring to a boil. Immediately remove from heat. Cover to keep warm.

Cook pasta in boiling water and salt in large uncovered pot or Dutch oven for 12 to 15 minutes, stirring occasionally, until tender but firm. Drain. Return to same pot.

Add squash mixture, mushroom mixture, Parmesan cheese and pine nuts. Toss. Transfer to serving platter. Top with crisped sage leaves. Makes 5 cups (1.25 L).

1 cup (250 mL): 295 Calories; 11.3 g Total Fat (6.2 g Mono, 3.4 g Poly, 0.9 g Sat); 0 mg Cholesterol; 43 g Carbohydrate; 3 g Fibre; 8 g Protein; 292 mg Sodium

Pictured on page 125.

Spinach Rotini

*Hearty combination of chickpeas, spinach
and pasta with sweet and spicy tomato sauce.*

Rotini pasta (about 8 oz., 225 g)	3 cups	750 mL
Boiling water	12 cups	3 L
Salt	1/2 tbsp.	7 mL
Olive (or cooking) oil	1 tbsp.	15 mL
Chopped onion	1 cup	250 mL
Garlic cloves, minced (or 1/2 tsp., 2 mL, powder)	2	2
Ground cinnamon	1 tsp.	5 mL
Ground coriander	1 tsp.	5 mL
Paprika	1 tsp.	5 mL
Cumin seed	1 tsp.	5 mL
Can of chickpeas (garbanzo beans), drained and rinsed	19 oz.	540 mL
Medium tomatoes, peeled (see Tip, page 63) and chopped	4	4
Chopped pitted dates	1/2 cup	125 mL
Chopped fresh thyme leaves	1 tbsp.	15 mL
Salt	1/2 tsp.	2 mL
Fresh spinach, stems removed, lightly packed	3 cups	750 mL

Cook pasta in boiling water and first amount of salt in large uncovered pot or Dutch oven for 12 to 15 minutes, stirring occasionally, until tender but firm. Drain. Return to same pot. Cover to keep warm.

Heat olive oil in large frying pan on medium. Add onion. Cook for 5 to 10 minutes, stirring often, until softened.

Add next 5 ingredients. Heat and stir for 1 to 2 minutes until fragrant.

Add next 5 ingredients. Stir. Bring to a boil. Reduce heat to medium-low. Cover. Simmer for about 20 minutes, stirring occasionally, until tomato is softened.

Add spinach. Heat and stir for 1 to 2 minutes until spinach is wilted. Add to pasta. Toss until coated. Makes 7 cups (1.75 mL). Serves 4.

1 serving: 500 Calories; 7.1 g Total Fat (3.1 g Mono, 1.7 g Poly, 0.9 g Sat); 0 mg Cholesterol; 96 g Carbohydrate; 10 g Fibre; 17 g Protein; 495 mg Sodium

Sun-Dried Tomato Pasta

An attractive and tasty dish full of tangy flavour and spicy heat.
Add as much pepper and Parmesan as you like.

Olive (or cooking) oil	2 tbsp.	30 mL
Garlic cloves, minced	4	4
Sun-dried tomatoes in oil, drained and chopped	1/2 cup	125 mL
Dried crushed chilies	1/4 – 1/2 tsp.	1 – 2 mL
Spaghetti	12 oz.	340 g
Boiling water	8 cups	2 L
Salt	1 tsp.	5 mL
Grated Parmesan cheese	1/2 cup	125 mL
Chopped fresh parsley	1/3 cup	75 mL
Coarse ground pepper	1/2 tsp.	2 mL

Heat olive oil in small frying pan on medium-low. Add garlic. Heat and stir for 1 to 2 minutes until fragrant.

Add sun-dried tomato and chilies. Heat and stir for about 2 minutes until tomato is hot. Remove from heat. Cover to keep warm.

Cook spaghetti in boiling water and salt in large uncovered pot or Dutch oven for 12 to 15 minutes, stirring occasionally, until tender but firm. Drain. Return to same pot. Add tomato mixture.

Add Parmesan cheese, parsley and pepper. Toss until spaghetti is coated. Makes 6 cups (1.5 L). Serves 4.

1 serving: 475 Calories; 14.3 g Total Fat (7.6 g Mono, 1.5 g Poly, 3.9 g Sat); 10 mg Cholesterol; 69 g Carbohydrate; 2 g Fibre; 17 g Protein; 296 mg Sodium

Paré Pointer

They're suffering from a modern sickness. They slipped a compact disc.

Tomato Peach Salsa

Vibrantly coloured, glistening salsa sure to whet any appetite! Serve with tortilla chips as an appetizer, or as a side with chicken, beef or lamb.

Lime juice	1 1/2 tsp.	7 mL
Peanut (or cooking) oil	1 1/2 tsp.	7 mL
Garlic clove, minced (or 1/4 tsp., 1 mL, powder)	1	1
Liquid honey	1/2 tsp.	2 mL
Chili powder	1/4 tsp.	1 mL
Salt	1/4 tsp.	1 mL
Pepper	1/8 tsp.	0.5 mL
Large tomato, quartered, seeds removed, diced	1	1
Large peach, peeled (see Tip, below) and pitted, diced	1	1
Chopped green onion	2 tbsp.	30 mL
Chopped fresh oregano leaves	1 tsp.	5 mL

Measure first 7 ingredients into medium bowl. Stir well.

Add remaining 4 ingredients. Toss until coated. Serve immediately. Makes 2 1/4 cups (550 mL).

1/4 cup (60 mL): 18 Calories; 0.9 g Total Fat (0.4 g Mono, 0.3 g Poly, 0.1 g Sat); 0 mg Cholesterol; 3 g Carbohydrate; 1 g Fibre; 0 g Protein; 68 mg Sodium

 tip

To peel peaches easily, blanch in boiling water for 30 to 60 seconds. Immediately plunge into cold water and remove skins.

Condiments

Herb Sauce

Mild white sauce flecked with fresh green herbs. Perfect with vegetables or fish.

Hard margarine (or butter)	2 tbsp.	30 mL
Finely chopped onion	1/2 cup	125 mL
Garlic clove, minced (or 1/4 tsp., 1 mL, powder)	1	1
All-purpose flour	2 tbsp.	30 mL
Dry white (or alcohol-free) wine	1/3 cup	75 mL
Milk	1 1/2 cups	375 mL
Chopped fresh chives (or 1 1/2 tsp., 7 mL, dried)	2 tbsp.	30 mL
Honey prepared mustard	1 tbsp.	15 mL
Finely chopped fresh parsley (or 3/4 tsp., 4 mL, flakes)	1 tbsp.	15 mL
Chopped fresh dill (or 3/4 tsp., 4 mL, dill weed)	1 tbsp.	15 mL
Salt	1/4 tsp.	1 mL

Melt margarine in medium saucepan on medium. Add onion. Cook for 5 to 10 minutes, stirring often, until softened.

Add garlic. Heat and stir for about 1 to 2 minutes until fragrant.

Add flour. Heat and stir for about 1 minute until blended. Add wine. Heat and stir until thickened.

Slowly add milk, stirring constantly, until mixture is boiling and thickened. Reduce heat to medium-low. Simmer, uncovered, for 5 minutes, stirring occasionally.

Add remaining 5 ingredients. Stir well. Makes about 2 cups (500 mL).

1/4 cup (60 mL): 70 Calories; 3.5 g Total Fat (2.1 g Mono, 0.4 g Poly, 0.9 g Sat); 2 mg Cholesterol; 6 g Carbohydrate; trace Fibre; 2 g Protein; 148 mg Sodium

Pictured on front cover.

Paré Pointer

An emergency brings out the best in people. It's the everyday living that brings out the worst.

Red Tartar Sauce

A spicy, tangy vegetable sauce. Wonderful served over grilled seafood or roasted chicken. Store in airtight container and keep in refrigerator for up to one week.

Garlic cloves (with skin)	2	2
Red medium pepper, halved	1	1
Large onions, cut into 1/2 inch (12 mm) thick slices	2	2
Olive (or cooking) oil	1 tsp.	5 mL
Mayonnaise	1/2 cup	125 mL
Chili sauce	1/3 cup	75 mL
Chopped dill pickles (or tangy dill relish)	1/4 cup	60 mL
Red wine vinegar	2 tsp.	10 mL
Paprika	1 tsp.	5 mL
Dried crushed chilies	1/8 tsp.	0.5 mL
Pepper, sprinkle		

Preheat electric grill for 5 minutes or gas barbecue to high. Loosely wrap garlic cloves in foil. Heat packet on grill (or broil in oven) for about 20 minutes, turning occasionally, until cloves are softened. Cool. Peel and discard skin. Transfer garlic to blender or food processor.

Cook pepper on greased grill (or broil in oven), skin-side down, for 10 to 12 minutes until skin is blackened and blistered. Transfer to small bowl. Cover with plastic wrap. Let sweat for about 15 minutes until cool enough to handle. Peel and discard skin and seeds, reserving any juices. Add roasted pepper and juices to garlic.

Brush onion slices with olive oil. Cook on greased grill for about 15 minutes, turning once, until softened. Add to pepper and garlic.

Add remaining 7 ingredients to blender or food processor. Pulse with on/off motion, scraping down sides, until coarsely chopped and well combined. Makes 2 cups (500 mL).

1 tbsp. (15 mL): 35 Calories; 3 g Total Fat (1.7 g Mono, 1 g Poly, 0.3 g Sat); 2 mg Cholesterol; 2 g Carbohydrate; trace Fibre; 0 g Protein; 71 mg Sodium

Yogurt Cucumber Side

Goes great with curries, roasts and barbecued meats. Or serve with Corn Roti, page 47, tortilla chips or pita bread as a refreshingly cool dip.

English cucumber (with peel)	1	1
Plain yogurt	2 1/2 cups	625 mL
Chopped fresh mint leaves	1/3 cup	75 mL
Lemon juice	1 tbsp.	15 mL
Garlic clove, minced (or 1/4 tsp., 1 mL, powder)	1	1
Ground cumin (optional)	1/2 tsp.	2 mL
Salt, just a pinch		

Cut cucumber in half lengthwise. Remove and discard seeds. Chop finely. Transfer to medium bowl.

Add remaining 6 ingredients. Stir well. Makes 3 3/4 cups (925 mL).

1/4 cup (60 mL): 31 Calories; 0.7 g Total Fat (0.2 g Mono, 0 g Poly, 0.4 g Sat); 3 mg Cholesterol; 4 g Carbohydrate; trace Fibre; 2 g Protein; 31 mg Sodium

Curry Butter

Sensational on grilled seafood! Use to add spicy flavour to chicken or your favourite vegetables.

Butter (or hard margarine), softened	1/2 cup	125 mL
Chopped fresh cilantro or parsley (or 1 1/2 tsp., 7 mL, dried)	2 tbsp.	30 mL
Curry powder	2 tsp.	10 mL
Liquid honey	1 tsp.	5 mL
Dried crushed chilies	1/4 tsp.	1 mL

Beat butter in small bowl until smooth and creamy.

Add remaining 4 ingredients. Beat well. Cover. Chill for about 1 hour until butter is firm but not hard. Makes 1/2 cup (125 mL) spread. Roll into 6 inch (15 cm) log. Wrap in plastic wrap and foil. May be stored in refrigerator for up to 5 days or in freezer for up to 3 months. Cuts into twelve 1/2 inch (12 mm) slices.

1 slice (2 tsp., 10 mL): 75 Calories; 8.2 g Total Fat (2.3 g Mono, 0.3 g Poly, 5.1 g Sat); 22 mg Cholesterol; 1 g Carbohydrate; trace Fibre; 0 g Protein; 84 mg Sodium

Garlic And Chive Butter

Exceptional garlic flavour. Excellent for making garlic toast or with fish, steak or vegetables.

Butter (or hard margarine), softened	1/2 cup	125 mL
Finely chopped fresh chives	1/4 cup	60 mL
Garlic cloves, minced (or 1/2 tsp., 2 mL, powder)	2	2
Lemon juice	1 tsp.	5 mL
Pepper, sprinkle		

Beat butter in small bowl until smooth and creamy.

Add remaining 4 ingredients. Beat well. Cover. Chill for about 1 hour until butter is firm but not hard. Makes 1/2 cup (125 mL) spread. Roll into 6 inch (15 cm) log. Wrap in plastic wrap and foil. May be stored in refrigerator for up to 5 days or in freezer for up to 3 months. Cuts into twelve 1/2 inch (12 mm) slices.

1 slice (2 tsp., 10 mL): 73 Calories; 8.1 g Total Fat (2.3 g Mono, 0.3 g Poly, 5.1 g Sat); 22 mg Cholesterol; 0 g Carbohydrate; 0 g Fibre; 0 g Protein; 83 mg Sodium

Pictured on front cover.

1. Megadarra, page 100
2. Herb Bread, page 49
3. Squash And Sage Pasta, page 117
4. Creamy Spinach Lasagne, page 102

Tomato Basil Butter

Perfect for melting over grilled chicken, lamb or beef.
Adds a savoury touch to zucchini and peppers or green beans.

Butter (or hard margarine), softened	1/2 cup	125 mL
Sun-dried tomatoes in oil, drained and finely chopped	2 tbsp.	30 mL
Finely chopped fresh basil	2 tbsp.	30 mL
Garlic clove, minced (or 1/4 tsp., 1 mL, powder)	1	1

Beat butter in small bowl until smooth and creamy.

Add remaining 3 ingredients. Beat well. Cover. Chill for about 1 hour until butter is firm but not hard. Makes 1/2 cup (125 mL) spread. Roll into 6 inch (15 cm) log. Wrap in plastic wrap and foil. May be stored in refrigerator for up to 5 days or in freezer for up to 3 months. Cuts into twelve 1/2 inch (12 mm) slices.

1 slice (2 tsp., 10 mL): 75 Calories; 8.3 g Total Fat (2.4 g Mono, 0.3 g Poly, 5.1 g Sat);
22 mg Cholesterol; 0 g Carbohydrate; 0 g Fibre; 0 g Protein; 86 mg Sodium

Pictured on page 53.

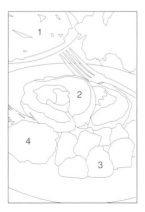

1. Glazed Roasted Carrots, page 106
2. Stuffed Pork Loin, page 93
3. Rosemary Sautéed Potatoes, page 109
4. Braised Red Cabbage, page 110

Props Courtesy Of: Pfaltzgraff Canada
Pier 1 Imports

Spiced Peach Topping

Tastes great warm or cold. Use as topping for ice cream or pancakes.
Can be frozen in airtight container or canned as Peach Conserve.

Fresh peaches, peeled (see Tip, page 120) and pitted, chopped	7 cups	1.75 L
Granulated sugar	4 cups	1 L
Lemon juice	1/2 cup	125 mL
Cinnamon stick (4 inches, 10 cm), broken in half	1	1
Whole cloves	5	5
Vanilla bean	1	1
Cheesecloth (4 inch, 10 cm, square)		

Measure peaches, sugar and lemon juice into large pot or Dutch oven. Stir.

Tie cinnamon stick halves, cloves and vanilla bean in cheesecloth. Add to peach mixture. Bring to a boil on medium. Reduce heat to medium-low. Simmer, uncovered, for about 65 minutes, stirring occasionally, until syrup is slightly thickened. Remove and discard spices and cheesecloth. Process mixture with hand blender for about 1 minute until thickened but still chunky. Makes 6 cups (1.5 L).

1/4 cup (60 mL): 160 Calories; 0.1 g Total Fat (0 g Mono, 0 g Poly, 0 g Sat); 0 mg Cholesterol; 42 g Carbohydrate; 1 g Fibre; 0 g Protein; 0 mg Sodium

Pictured on page 53.

PEACH CONSERVE: Bring Spiced Peach Topping to a boil on medium. Reduce heat to medium-low. Simmer, uncovered, for about 1 hour, stirring occasionally, until mixture gels. To test, remove peach mixture from heat. Transfer small amount to ice-cold plate. Place in freezer for 2 minutes. If mixture gels, it is ready for canning. If not, return peach mixture to heat and simmer for 10 minutes. Retest for gelling. Fill 6 hot sterile 1/2 pint (250 mL) jars to within 1/4 inch (6 mm) of top. Wipe rims of jars. Place sterile metal lids on jars and screw on metal bands fingertip tight. Do not over-tighten. Process in boiling water bath for 10 minutes (see Note). Makes 6 cups (1.5 L).

Note: Processing time is for elevations 1001 to 3000 feet (306 to 915 m) above sea level. Make adjustment for elevation in your area if necessary.

Bread And Butter Pickles

Good sweet and sour blend in this versatile pickle. Use a crinkle cutter
to make cucumber slices more attractive.

English cucumbers (with peel), about 2 lbs. (900 g), cut into 1/4 inch (6 mm) thick slices	2	2
Thinly sliced onion	1 1/2 cups	375 mL
Coarse (pickling) salt	1/4 cup	60 mL
Apple cider vinegar	1 1/2 cups	375 mL
Granulated sugar	1 1/2 cups	375 mL
Yellow mustard seed	2 tbsp.	30 mL
Cumin seed, toasted (see Tip, page 33)	2 tsp.	10 mL
Celery seed	1 tsp.	5 mL
Turmeric	3/4 tsp.	4 mL

Combine cucumber, onion and coarse salt in extra-large bowl. Place plate, large enough to fit snugly into bowl, directly on top of cucumber mixture. Place heavy cans on top of plate to apply pressure. Let stand at room temperature for 4 hours. Remove cans and plate. Rinse cucumber mixture. Drain well.

Measure remaining 6 ingredients into large saucepan. Heat and stir on medium until sugar is dissolved. Add cucumber mixture. Stir. Bring to a boil. Immediately remove from heat. Fill 6 hot sterile 1/2 pint (250 mL) jars to within 1/2 inch (12 mm) of top. Wipe rims of jars. Place sterile metal lids on jars and screw on metal bands fingertip tight. Do not over-tighten. Process in boiling water bath for 10 minutes (see Note). Remove jars. Cool. Makes 6 cups (1.5 L).

1/4 cup (60 mL): 68 Calories; 0.4 g Total Fat (0.2 g Mono, 0.1 g Poly, 0 g Sat); 0 mg Cholesterol; 17 g Carbohydrate; 1 g Fibre; 1 g Protein; 1180 mg Sodium

Pictured on page 89.

Note: Processing time is for elevations 1001 to 3000 feet (306 to 915 m) above sea level. Make adjustment for elevation in your area if necessary.

Tomato Chutney

Sweet and sour flavours are delicious served alongside
your favourite roasted meats.

Tomatoes, peeled (see Tip, page 63) and chopped	5 1/2 cups	1.4 L
Chopped onion	3 cups	750 mL
Golden raisins	1 1/2 cups	375 mL
Large cooking apples (such as McIntosh), peeled and cored, diced	4	4
Brown sugar, packed	3 cups	750 mL
Malt vinegar	2 cups	500 mL
Can of tomato paste	5 1/2 oz.	156 mL
Worcestershire sauce	2 tbsp.	30 mL
Dry mustard	1 tbsp.	15 mL
Ground ginger	1 tbsp.	15 mL
Coarse (pickling) salt	1 tbsp.	15 mL
Whole cloves	6	6

Combine all 12 ingredients in large pot or Dutch oven. Heat and stir on medium until sugar is dissolved. Bring to a boil. Reduce heat to medium-low. Simmer, uncovered, for about 1 1/2 hours, stirring occasionally, until slightly thickened. Fill 12 hot sterile 1/2 pint (250 mL) jars to within 1/2 inch (12 mm) of top. Wipe rims of jars. Place sterile metal lids on jars and screw on metal bands fingertip tight. Do not over-tighten. Process in boiling water bath for 15 minutes (see Note). Remove jars. Cool. Mixture will thicken more while cooling. Makes 12 cups (3 L).

1 tbsp. (15 mL): 22 Calories; 0.1 g Total Fat (0 g Mono, 0 g Poly, 0 g Sat); 0 mg Cholesterol; 6 g Carbohydrate; trace Fibre; 0 g Protein; 40 mg Sodium

Note: Processing time is for elevations 1001 to 3000 feet (306 to 915 m) above sea level. Make adjustment for elevation in your area if necessary.

Paré Pointer

A lot of doctors scorn acupuncture. They would rather stick you with their bill.

Condiments

Mango Chutney

Zippy fruit and spice combination makes this golden chutney a great addition to roasted meats or samosas. Don't wait for a special occasion—great any time!

Peeled, chopped firm mango (about 4 medium)	5 cups	1.25 L
Chopped onion	3 cups	750 mL
Large cooking apples (such as McIntosh), peeled and cored, diced	3	3
Golden raisins	1 1/2 cups	375 mL
Chopped pitted dates	2/3 cup	150 mL
Small tomatoes, chopped	3	3
White vinegar	3 cups	750 mL
Granulated sugar	2 cups	500 mL
Finely grated, peeled gingerroot	1 tbsp.	15 mL
Garlic cloves, minced	4	4
Curry powder	1 tbsp.	15 mL
Coarse (pickling) salt	1 tbsp.	15 mL
Dried crushed chilies	2 tsp.	10 mL

Measure all 13 ingredients into large pot or Dutch oven. Heat and stir on medium until sugar is dissolved. Bring to a boil. Reduce heat to medium-low. Simmer, uncovered, for about 1 1/2 hours, stirring occasionally, until slightly thickened. Fill 11 hot sterile 1/2 pint (250 mL) jars to within 1/2 inch (12 mm) of top. Wipe rims of jars. Place sterile metal lids on jars and screw on metal bands fingertip tight. Do not over-tighten. Process in boiling water bath for 15 minutes (see Note). Remove jars. Cool. Mixture will thicken more while cooling. Makes 11 cups (2.75 L).

1 tbsp. (15 mL): 43 Calories; 0.1 g Total Fat (0 g Mono, 0 g Poly, 0 g Sat); 0 mg Cholesterol; 11 g Carbohydrate; 1 g Fibre; 0 g Protein; 79 mg Sodium

Pictured on page 143.

Note: Processing time is for elevations 1001 to 3000 feet (306 to 915 m) above sea level. Make adjustment for elevation in your area if necessary.

Spiced-Up Beet Relish

Allspice adds a delicate, interesting flavour to ham and pork.
Also good with egg dishes. Tasty!

Finely chopped onion	3 cups	750 mL
Grated fresh beets (about 5 large)	2 1/2 cups	625 mL
White vinegar	1 1/4 cups	300 mL
Granulated sugar	1 cup	250 mL
Yellow mustard seed	2 tbsp.	30 mL
Coarse (pickling) salt	2 tsp.	10 mL
Ground allspice	1 1/2 tsp.	7 mL
Dried crushed chilies	1 tsp.	5 mL

Combine all 8 ingredients in large pot or Dutch oven. Heat and stir on medium-high until sugar is dissolved. Bring to a boil. Reduce heat to medium. Boil, uncovered, for about 30 minutes, stirring occasionally, until beets are tender and liquid is almost evaporated. Fill 6 hot sterile 1/2 pint (250 mL) jars to within 1/2 inch (12 mm) of top. Wipe rims of jars. Place sterile metal lids on jars and screw on metal bands fingertip tight. Do not over-tighten. Process in boiling water bath for 10 minutes (see Note). Remove jars. Cool. Makes 6 cups (1.5 L).

1 tbsp. (15 mL): 13 Calories; 0.1 g Total Fat (0.1 g Mono, 0 g Poly, 0 g Sat); 0 mg Cholesterol; 3 g Carbohydrate; trace Fibre; 0 g Protein; 51 mg Sodium

Note: Processing time is for elevations 1001 to 3000 feet (306 to 915 m) above sea level. Make adjustment for elevation in your area if necessary.

Tarragon Garlic Vinegar

Use this flavourful dressing in Springy Pasta Salad, page 57, or
Seashell Pasta Salad, page 61. Great on greens, too, with a dash of olive oil.

White wine vinegar	2 cups	500 mL
Whole black peppercorns, crushed (see Tip, page 96)	5	5
Fresh tarragon leaves	4	4
Garlic cloves, chopped	3	3
Fresh tarragon leaves	2	2

(continued on next page)

Measure first 4 ingredients into jar with tight-fitting lid. Shake gently. Let stand at room temperature for 24 hours to blend flavours. Strain vinegar mixture through sieve into 4 cup (1 L) liquid measure. Discard solids.

Place second amount of tarragon in decorative jar or cruet. Pour vinegar mixture over tarragon to fill jar. Cover. Chill. May be stored in refrigerator for up to 3 months. Makes 2 cups (500 mL).

1 tbsp. (15 mL): 3 Calories; 0 g Total Fat (0 g Mono, 0 g Poly, 0 g Sat); 0 mg Cholesterol; 1 g Carbohydrate; 0 g Fibre; 0 g Protein; 0 mg Sodium

Pictured on front cover.

Tomato Relish

Goes well with beef, pork or chicken. Try it on a hamburger!

Medium tomatoes, peeled (see Tip, page 63) and chopped (about 2 1/2 lbs., 1.1 kg)	8	8
Finely chopped onion	2 cups	500 mL
Brown sugar, packed	1 1/2 cups	375 mL
Malt vinegar	1 cup	250 mL
Tomato paste (see Tip, page 87)	1/4 cup	60 mL
Curry powder	1 1/2 tbsp.	25 mL
Dry mustard	1 1/2 tbsp.	25 mL
Coarse (pickling) salt	2 tsp.	10 mL

Combine all 8 ingredients in large pot or Dutch oven. Heat and stir on medium until sugar is dissolved. Bring to a boil. Reduce heat to medium-low. Simmer, uncovered, for 40 minutes, stirring occasionally. Increase heat to medium. Boil for about 20 minutes, stirring occasionally, until slightly thickened and liquid is almost evaporated. Fill 6 hot sterile 1/2 pint (250 mL) jars to within 1/2 inch (12 mm) of top. Wipe rims of jars. Place sterile metal lids on jars and screw on metal bands fingertip tight. Do not over-tighten. Process in boiling water bath for 10 minutes (see Note). Remove jars. Cool. Makes 6 cups (1.5 L).

1 tbsp. (15 mL): 19 Calories; 0.1 g Total Fat (0 g Mono, 0 g Poly, 0 g Sat); 0 mg Cholesterol; 5 g Carbohydrate; trace Fibre; 0 g Protein; 50 mg Sodium

Pictured on page 89.

Note: Processing time is for elevations 1001 to 3000 feet (306 to 915 m) above sea level. Make adjustment for elevation in your area if necessary.

Corn Relish

Sweet and crunchy, colourful relish. Perfect for barbecue season.

White vinegar	1 1/2 cups	375 mL
Diced red pepper	1 cup	250 mL
Diced celery	1 cup	250 mL
Diced onion	1 cup	250 mL
Finely chopped cabbage	1 cup	250 mL
Granulated sugar	1 cup	250 mL
Yellow mustard seed	1 tbsp.	15 mL
Dry mustard	2 tsp.	10 mL
Turmeric	2 tsp.	10 mL
Salt	1 tbsp.	15 mL
Cans of kernel corn, drained (12 oz., 341 mL, each)	2	2
Water	1/2 cup	125 mL
All-purpose flour	1/4 cup	60 mL

Measure first 10 ingredients into large pot or Dutch oven. Heat and stir on medium until sugar is dissolved. Bring to a boil. Reduce heat to medium-low. Simmer, uncovered, for 25 minutes, stirring occasionally.

Add corn. Stir. Simmer for 10 minutes, stirring occasionally.

Stir water into flour in small bowl until smooth. Slowly add to corn mixture, stirring constantly, until well combined. Simmer, uncovered, for 10 to 15 minutes, stirring occasionally, until thickened. Fill 5 hot sterile 1/2 pint (250 mL) jars to within 1/2 inch (12 mm) of top. Wipe rims of jars. Place sterile metal lids on jars and screw on metal bands fingertip tight. Do not over-tighten. Process in boiling water bath for 10 minutes (see Note). Remove jars. Cool. Makes 5 cups (1.25 L).

1 tbsp. (15 mL): 20 Calories; 0.1 g Total Fat (0.1 g Mono, 0 g Poly, 0 g Sat); 0 mg Cholesterol; 5 g Carbohydrate; trace Fibre; 0 g Protein; 104 mg Sodium

Pictured on page 89.

Note: Processing time is for elevations 1001 to 3000 feet (306 to 915 m) above sea level. Make adjustment for elevation in your area if necessary.

Condiments

West Indian Relish

Tender-crisp vegetables mingled with exotic spices make a great addition to burgers or sandwiches.

Apple cider vinegar	1/4 cup	60 mL
Granulated sugar	2 tbsp.	30 mL
Ground cardamom	3/4 tsp.	4 mL
Ground cumin	1/2 tsp.	2 mL
Salt	1/8 tsp.	0.5 mL
Pepper	1/4 tsp.	1 mL
Small English cucumbers (with peel), quartered lengthwise, seeds removed, diced	2	2
Red medium pepper, seeds and ribs removed, diced	1/2	1/2
Diced onion	1/2 cup	125 mL
Fresh chili pepper, seeds and ribs removed, diced (see Tip, below)	2 tsp.	10 mL

Measure first 6 ingredients into large saucepan. Heat and stir on medium until sugar is dissolved and spices are fragrant.

Add remaining 4 ingredients. Stir. Bring to a boil. Reduce heat to medium-low. Simmer, uncovered, for 10 to 12 minutes, stirring occasionally, until vegetables are tender-crisp and liquid is almost evaporated. Transfer to blender or food processor. Pulse with on/off motion for about 30 seconds until finely diced. May be stored in airtight container in refrigerator for up to 3 days. Makes 2 cups (500 mL).

1 tbsp. (15 mL): 8 Calories; 0.1 g Total Fat (0 g Mono, 0 g Poly, 0 g Sat); 0 mg Cholesterol; 2 g Carbohydrate; trace Fibre; 0 g Protein; 10 mg Sodium

Pictured on page 53.

 tip *Chilies and hot peppers contain capsaicin in the seeds and ribs. Removing the seeds and ribs will reduce the heat. Wear rubber gloves when handling chilies or peppers and avoid touching your eyes. Wash your hands well afterwards.*

Ginger Cookies

The flavour of ginger is strong and delicious. A hard cookie that's great for dunking!

Hard margarine (or butter)	1/3 cup	75 mL
Brown sugar, packed	1/3 cup	75 mL
Golden corn syrup	1/3 cup	75 mL
All-purpose flour	1 1/3 cups	325 mL
Minced crystallized ginger	1/4 cup	60 mL
Ground ginger	1 tbsp.	15 mL
Ground cinnamon	1 tsp.	5 mL
Baking soda	3/4 tsp.	4 mL
Salt, just a pinch		

Measure first 3 ingredients into small saucepan. Heat and stir on medium until margarine is melted. Remove from heat. Let stand until cooled to room temperature.

Combine remaining 6 ingredients in large bowl. Add margarine mixture. Stir well. Roll into balls, using 2 tsp. (10 mL) for each. Arrange, about 1 1/2 inches (3.8 cm) apart, on greased cookie sheets. Flatten slightly. Bake in 350°F (175°C) oven for 8 to 10 minutes until edges are golden. Let stand on cookie sheets for 5 minutes. Loosen cookies with lifter. Let stand on cookie sheets until cooled completely. Makes about 30 cookies.

1 cookie: 63 Calories; 2.2 g Total Fat (1.4 g Mono, 0.2 g Poly, 0.5 g Sat); 0 mg Cholesterol; 10 g Carbohydrate; trace Fibre; 1 g Protein; 63 mg Sodium

Caribbean Bananas

Comforting blend of rum and spice in a warm, buttery dessert. Serve with whipped cream, ice cream or plain yogurt.

Medium bananas (slightly green)	6	6
Lime juice	1 tbsp.	15 mL
Brown sugar, packed	1/3 cup	75 mL
Ground allspice	1 tsp.	5 mL
Ground ginger	3/4 tsp.	4 mL

(continued on next page)

Spiced rum	2 tbsp.	30 mL
Hard margarine (or butter)	2 tbsp.	30 mL

Cut each banana in half crosswise. Cut each portion in half lengthwise for a total of 24 pieces. Arrange in single layer in greased 3 quart (3 L) casserole. Brush with lime juice.

Combine next 3 ingredients in small bowl. Sprinkle over bananas. Bake, uncovered, in 400°F (205°C) oven for 13 to 15 minutes until bananas are softened but not mushy.

Heat rum in small saucepan on medium until just warm. Carefully ignite rum. When flames subside, add margarine. Stir until margarine is melted. Drizzle over bananas. Serves 6.

1 serving: 202 Calories; 4.5 g Total Fat (2.6 g Mono, 0.5 g Poly, 1 g Sat); 0 mg Cholesterol; 40 g Carbohydrate; 2 g Fibre; 1 g Protein; 52 mg Sodium

Caraway Seed Pound Cake

Moist cake with an occasional burst of caraway. Serve with tea or coffee.

Hard margarine (or butter), softened	1 cup	250 mL
Granulated sugar	1 cup	250 mL
Vanilla	1 tsp.	5 mL
Large eggs	4	4
All-purpose flour	1 1/2 cups	375 mL
Baking powder	2 tsp.	10 mL
Caraway seed, toasted (see Note)	1 1/2 tsp.	7 mL

Beat margarine, sugar and vanilla in medium bowl until light and creamy.

Add eggs, 1 at a time, beating well after each addition.

Combine flour, baking powder and caraway seed in small bowl. Add to margarine mixture. Stir. Spread evenly in greased 8 inch (20 cm) springform pan. Bake in 350°F (175°C) oven for about 45 minutes until wooden pick inserted in centre comes out clean. Let stand in pan for 10 minutes before removing to wire rack to cool. Cuts into 12 wedges.

1 wedge: 299 Calories; 18 g Total Fat (11.2 g Mono, 1.9 g Poly, 3.9 g Sat); 72 mg Cholesterol; 31 g Carbohydrate; 1 g Fibre; 4 g Protein; 272 mg Sodium

Note: Toast caraway seed in small ungreased frying pan on medium until they make a snapping sound.

Peach Kulfi

An Indian dessert, similar to ice cream, but icier and not overly sweet.
Refreshingly light. A great end to a spicy meal.

Granulated sugar	1/3 cup	75 mL
Cornstarch	2 tbsp.	30 mL
Cans of evaporated milk (13 1/2 oz., 385 mL, each)	2	2
Whole green cardamom, bruised (see Tip, page 83)	6	6
Cinnamon stick (4 inches, 10 cm)	1	1
Egg yolks (large)	2	2
Can of frozen concentrated peach punch, thawed (1 1/2 cups, 375 mL)	12 1/2 oz.	355 mL
Egg whites (large)	2	2
Pistachios, shelled and skinned	1/3 cup	75 mL

Measure sugar and cornstarch into large saucepan. Stir. Slowly add evaporated milk, stirring constantly, until smooth. Add cardamom and cinnamon stick. Heat and stir on medium for about 10 minutes until boiling and slightly thickened. Remove from heat.

Beat egg yolks with fork in small bowl. Add 1 tbsp. (15 mL) milk mixture to egg yolks. Stir well. Slowly add egg yolk mixture to milk mixture, stirring constantly. Heat and stir on medium for 2 to 3 minutes until thickened. Remove from heat. Remove and discard cardamom and cinnamon stick.

Add peach punch. Stir. Cover with plastic wrap directly on surface to prevent skin from forming. Let stand for about 30 minutes until cooled to room temperature.

Beat egg whites in large bowl until stiff peaks form.

Fold cooled milk mixture and pistachios into egg whites until no white streaks remain. Spread evenly in waxed paper-lined 9 x 13 inch (22 x 33 cm) pan. Cover with foil. Freeze overnight until firm. Invert onto cutting surface. Remove waxed paper. Cut into 3 rows lengthwise and 4 rows crosswise, for a total of 12 rectangles. Cut each rectangle in half diagonally, for a total of 24 triangles. Serves 12.

1 serving: 218 Calories; 8.4 g Total Fat (3.3 g Mono, 0.7 g Poly, 3.8 g Sat); 56 mg Cholesterol; 30 g Carbohydrate; trace Fibre; 6 g Protein; 87 mg Sodium

Pictured on page 143.

Vanilla Bean Fruit Salad

Vibrant! Delicious! Sweet vanilla with sparkling wine,
mint and fresh fruit flavours.

VANILLA SYRUP

Granulated sugar	1 cup	250 mL
Water	1/2 cup	125 mL
Vanilla bean	1	1
Finely grated lime zest	1/2 tsp.	2 mL
Fresh pineapple, peeled and cored, cut into bite-size pieces (about 5 cups, 1.25 L)	1	1
Cubed cantaloupe	2 cups	500 mL
Kiwifruit, peeled and quartered	4	4
Quartered fresh strawberries	3 cups	750 mL
Sparkling white (or rosé) wine (or white grape juice)	1/2 cup	125 mL
Fresh mint leaves, torn	12	12
Fresh mint sprigs, for garnish	8	8

Vanilla Syrup: Combine sugar and water in small saucepan. Split vanilla bean in half lengthwise. Scrape seeds from pod into sugar mixture. Add pod halves. Heat and stir on medium for about 4 minutes until sugar is dissolved. Increase heat to medium-high. Brush side of saucepan with damp pastry brush to dissolve any sugar crystals. Boil for about 5 minutes, without stirring, until syrup is slightly thickened. Remove from heat.

Add lime zest. Stir. Let stand for 10 minutes. Pour into extra-large bowl. Cover. Chill for 1 hour. Remove and discard pod halves. Leave seeds in syrup. Makes about 1 cup (250 mL) syrup.

Add pineapple, cantaloupe and kiwifruit to syrup. Stir until coated. Cover. Chill for at least 3 hours, stirring occasionally.

Add strawberries, wine and torn mint leaves. Stir. Makes about 9 1/2 cups (2.4 L) fruit salad.

Divide and spoon into 8 dessert bowls. Garnish with mint sprigs. Serves 8.

1 serving: 208 Calories; 0.9 g Total Fat (0.1 g Mono, 0.3 g Poly, 0 g Sat); 0 mg Cholesterol; 52 g Carbohydrate; 4 g Fibre; 2 g Protein; 8 mg Sodium

Pictured on front cover.

Elegant Bread Pudding

Light, moist pudding with delicate balance of fruit and spice. Wonderful vanilla flavour. Garnish with whipped cream and dried apricots.

Finely chopped dried apricots	1/2 cup	125 mL
Golden raisins	1/2 cup	125 mL
Almond-flavoured liqueur (such as Amaretto)	3 tbsp.	50 mL
Apricot jam	1/3 cup	75 mL
French bread slices, 1/2 inch (12 mm) thick	12	12
Homogenized milk	4 cups	1 L
Granulated sugar	3/4 cup	175 mL
Vanilla bean	1	1
Large eggs	4	4
Salt	1/8 tsp.	0.5 mL

Combine apricot, raisins and liqueur in small bowl. Let stand for 15 minutes. Spoon 1/2 of apricot mixture into greased 2 1/2 quart (2.5 L) casserole. Spread evenly.

Spread apricot jam on 1 side of each bread slice. Cut each slice into 3 equal pieces. Arrange pieces, jam-side up and slightly overlapping, in casserole. Spoon remaining apricot mixture evenly over bread.

Measure milk and sugar into medium saucepan. Split vanilla bean in half lengthwise. Scrape seeds from pod into milk mixture. Add pod halves. Heat and stir on medium until bubbles form around edge and sugar is dissolved. Remove from heat. Let stand for 20 minutes. Remove and discard pod halves.

Beat eggs and salt with fork in large bowl. Slowly add milk mixture, beating constantly, until well combined. Pour evenly over bread. Let stand for 10 minutes. Cover. Place casserole in large pan. Carefully pour boiling water into pan until water comes halfway up side of casserole. Bake in 325°F (160°C) oven for 1 1/2 hours. Remove cover. Bake for about 20 minutes until knife inserted in centre of pudding comes out clean. Carefully remove casserole from water in pan. Let stand on wire rack for 15 minutes. Serves 8.

1 serving: 373 Calories; 7.7 g Total Fat (2.6 g Mono, 0.7 g Poly, 3.6 g Sat); 125 mg Cholesterol; 64 g Carbohydrate; 2 g Fibre; 10 g Protein; 301 mg Sodium

Pictured on page 144.

Lavender Crème Brûlée

Rich, velvety chocolate with subtle lavender flavour. An elegant,
decadent dessert!

Whipping cream	2 cups	500 mL
Dried lavender	1 tsp.	5 mL
Cheesecloth (4 inch, 10 cm, square)		
White chocolate baking squares (1 oz., 28 g, each), chopped	6	6
Granulated sugar	1/4 cup	60 mL
Egg yolks (large), fork-beaten	6	6
Vanilla	1/2 tsp.	2 mL
Granulated sugar	3 tbsp.	50 mL

Grease six 1/2 cup (125 mL) ovenproof ramekins. Place in 9 × 13 inch
(22 × 33 cm) pan. Measure whipping cream into heavy medium saucepan.
Tie lavender in cheesecloth. Add to whipping cream. Heat on medium until
bubbles form around edge. Remove from heat. Cover. Let stand for
5 minutes. Press cheesecloth with back of spoon against side of saucepan
to squeeze out any liquid. Remove and discard cheesecloth and lavender.

Add chocolate and first amount of sugar. Stir until chocolate is melted.

Add egg yolk and vanilla. Beat with whisk until well combined. Divide and
pour into prepared ramekins. Spread evenly. Carefully pour boiling water
into pan until water comes halfway up sides of ramekins. Bake in 300°F
(150°C) oven for 40 to 45 minutes until almost set. Remove ramekins from
water to wire rack to cool completely. Cover. Chill for at least 6 hours.

Divide and sprinkle second amount of sugar evenly over top of each. Broil
on top rack in oven for about 3 minutes until sugar is bubbling and
browned. Remove from oven. Let stand for 5 minutes before serving.
Serves 6.

1 serving: 523 Calories; 40.6 g Total Fat (12.5 g Mono, 1.8 g Poly, 23.4 g Sat); 319 mg Cholesterol;
35 g Carbohydrate; 0 g Fibre; 6 g Protein; 63 mg Sodium

Paré Pointer

When the doctor told the young man his sickness was hereditary,
he told the doctor to send the bill to his father.

Cinnamon Anise Oranges

Use a sweet wine such as Riesling, Ehrenfelser or Spätlese to make these.
Cinnamon, star anise and vanilla create flavour and aroma in this light dessert.
Garnish with a fresh cinnamon stick.

Sweet white wine	1 1/2 cups	375 mL
Granulated sugar	1/2 cup	125 mL
Water	3 tbsp.	50 mL
Star anise	4	4
Cinnamon stick (4 inches, 10 cm)	1	1
Vanilla bean, split lengthwise	1	1
Orange-flavoured liqueur (such as Grand Marnier)	2 tbsp.	30 mL
Small oranges, peeled and white pith removed, halved crosswise	8	8

Combine first 6 ingredients in medium saucepan. Bring to a boil on medium-high. Reduce heat to medium. Simmer, uncovered, for 10 minutes, without stirring. Remove from heat. Cool.

Add liqueur. Stir. Pour into large bowl. Add oranges. Stir until coated. Cover. Chill for at least 6 hours, stirring occasionally. Remove and discard star anise, cinnamon stick and vanilla bean halves before serving. Serves 8.

1 serving: 153 Calories; 0.2 g Total Fat (0 g Mono, 0 g Poly, 0 g Sat); 0 mg Cholesterol; 29 g Carbohydrate; 2 g Fibre; 1 g Protein; 3 mg Sodium

Pictured on page 144.

1. Peach Kulfi, page 138
2. Spicy Naan Bread, page 42
3. Saffron Lassi, page 32
4. Mango Chutney, page 131
5. Beef Madras Curry, page 84

Props Courtesy Of: Casa Bugatti
Linens 'N Things
Pier 1 Imports

Ginger Basil Sorbet

*Very refreshing and cleansing. Try it after dinner with
a splash of pear or apple-flavoured liqueur.*

Water	5 cups	1.25 L
Granulated sugar	2 1/2 cups	625 mL
Finely grated, peeled gingerroot	1/3 cup	75 mL
Fresh basil leaves, packed	1/4 cup	60 mL
Lime juice	1/4 cup	60 mL

Combine water and sugar in medium saucepan. Bring to a boil on
medium-high. Reduce heat to medium. Boil for 5 minutes. Remove
from heat.

Add ginger and basil. Stir. Let stand for 10 minutes. Strain through sieve
into large bowl. Discard solids.

Add lime juice. Stir. Cover. Chill for at least 3 hours. Pour into ice cream
maker (see Note). Freeze according to manufacturer's instructions. Makes
6 cups (1.5 L).

*1/2 cup (125 mL): 174 Calories; 0 g Total Fat (0 g Mono, 0 g Poly, 0 g Sat); 0 mg Cholesterol;
45 g Carbohydrate; trace Fibre; 0 g Protein; 1 mg Sodium*

Note: If you don't have an ice cream maker, pour sorbet into 9 x 13 inch
(22 x 33 cm) baking dish to freeze. Stir mixture every hour for 4 hours.
Sorbet will have a flakier texture, but flavour will not be affected.

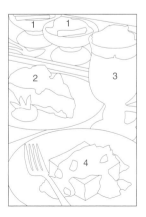

1. Cinnamon Anise Oranges, page 142
2. Elegant Bread Pudding, page 140
3. Special Spiced Coffee, page 34
4. Fall Gingerbread, page 146

Props Courtesy Of: Canhome Global
Pfaltzgraff Canada

Fall Gingerbread

Although the ingredient list is long, this recipe is quick, easy and so good!
A satisfying, aromatic dessert, best served warm.

GINGERBREAD

Hard margarine (or butter), softened	1/4 cup	60 mL
Granulated sugar	1/3 cup	75 mL
Large egg	1	1
All-purpose flour	1 1/2 cups	375 mL
Fancy (mild) molasses	1/3 cup	75 mL
Buttermilk (or reconstituted from powder)	1/4 cup	60 mL
Ground ginger	1 tsp.	5 mL
Ground cinnamon	3/4 tsp.	4 mL
Baking powder	1/2 tsp.	2 mL
Baking soda	1/2 tsp.	2 mL
Salt	1/2 tsp.	2 mL
Ground nutmeg	1/4 tsp.	1 mL

MIXED FRUIT SAUCE

Chopped mixed dried fruit (such as apricots, prunes and cranberries), packed	1 cup	250 mL
Boiling water	2 cups	500 mL
Lemon juice	1 tbsp.	15 mL
Granulated sugar	1/2 cup	125 mL
Cornstarch	1 tbsp.	15 mL
Ground ginger	1/4 tsp.	1 mL
Ground cinnamon	1/4 tsp.	1 mL

Gingerbread: Beat margarine and sugar on medium in large bowl until light and creamy. Add egg. Beat well.

Add next 9 ingredients. Beat for about 2 minutes until smooth. Spoon into greased 9 x 9 inch (22 x 22 cm) pan. Spread evenly. Bake in 350°F (175°C) oven for 30 to 35 minutes until wooden pick inserted in centre comes out clean. Cuts into 12 pieces.

Mixed Fruit Sauce: Measure fruit into medium saucepan. Pour boiling water over top. Cover. Let stand for 15 minutes.

Add lemon juice. Stir. Bring to a boil on medium.

(continued on next page)

Desserts

Combine remaining 4 ingredients in small bowl. Slowly add to fruit mixture, stirring constantly, until boiling and thickened. Makes 2 3/4 cups (675 mL) sauce. Spoon over individual servings of warm gingerbread. Serves 12.

1 piece gingerbread with 3 tbsp. (50 mL) fruit sauce: 212 Calories; 4.8 g Total Fat (2.9 g Mono, 0.5 g Poly, 1 g Sat); 18 mg Cholesterol; 41 g Carbohydrate; 1 g Fibre; 3 g Protein; 178 mg Sodium

Pictured on page 144.

Honey Creamed Rice

Subtly spiced. Sweet raisins, honey and toasted nuts make this thick, creamy rice pudding especially good. Serve warm or cold.

Homogenized milk	6 cups	1.5 L
Liquid honey	1/4 cup	60 mL
Short grain white rice	1 cup	250 mL
Golden raisins	1/3 cup	75 mL
Ground cardamom	1/4 tsp.	1 mL
Ground ginger	1/4 tsp.	1 mL
Salt	1/4 tsp.	1 mL
Liquid honey	2 tbsp.	30 mL
Pecan pieces, toasted (see Tip, page 33)	2 tbsp.	30 mL
Pine nuts, toasted (see Tip, page 33)	2 tbsp.	30 mL

Measure milk and first amount of honey into large heavy saucepan. Heat and stir on medium until boiling.

Add next 5 ingredients. Reduce heat to medium-low. Simmer, uncovered, for about 55 minutes, stirring occasionally, until rice is tender and mixture is creamy and slightly thickened. Mixture will thicken as it cools.

Add second amount of honey. Stir. Makes 5 cups (1.25 L).

Transfer to large serving bowl. Sprinkle with pecans and pine nuts. Serves 8.

1 serving: 282 Calories; 6.6 g Total Fat (1.9 g Mono, 0.3 g Poly, 4.1 g Sat); 26 mg Cholesterol; 48 g Carbohydrate; trace Fibre; 8 g Protein; 171 mg Sodium

Paré Pointer

Nature is always referred to as a woman because there is no way to tell how old it is.

Desserts

Nutmeg Cheesecake

The taste of nutmeg and a hint of orange. Creamy and rich!

CRUST		
Finely crushed vanilla wafers (about 53 wafers)	2 cups	500 mL
Ground nutmeg	1/2 tsp.	2 mL
Ground ginger	1/2 tsp.	2 mL
Hard margarine (or butter), melted	1/2 cup	125 mL

FILLING		
Blocks of cream cheese (8 oz., 250 g, each), softened	2	2
Granulated sugar	2/3 cup	150 mL
Large eggs	4	4
Orange juice	2 tbsp.	30 mL
Finely grated orange zest	1 tbsp.	15 mL
Ground nutmeg	1/2 tsp.	2 mL
Salt	1/4 tsp.	1 mL

Whipped topping, for garnish
Mandarin orange segments, drained
  (for garnish)
Ground nutmeg, sprinkle

Crust: Combine first 4 ingredients in medium bowl until well mixed. Press mixture firmly into bottom and 1 inch (2.5 cm) up side of greased 9 inch (22 cm) springform pan. Chill for 30 minutes.

Filling: Beat cream cheese and sugar in large bowl until smooth. Add eggs, 1 at a time, beating after each addition until just combined.

Add next 4 ingredients. Beat well. Pour over prepared crust. Spread evenly. Bake in 325°F (160°C) oven for about 50 minutes until centre is almost set. Run knife around inside edge of pan to allow cheesecake to settle evenly. Let stand in pan on wire rack until cooled completely. Cover. Chill for at least 8 hours or overnight.

Garnish individual servings with whipped topping and orange segments. Sprinkle nutmeg lightly over top of each. Cuts into 10 wedges.

1 wedge: 423 Calories; 31.8 g Total Fat (13 g Mono, 2.5 g Poly, 14.2 g Sat); 151 mg Cholesterol; 29 g Carbohydrate; trace Fibre; 7 g Protein; 398 mg Sodium

Pictured on page 107.

Cinnamon Coffee Cake

Light and tender. Served warm.

Hard margarine (or butter), softened	1/2 cup	125 mL
Granulated sugar	2/3 cup	150 mL
Vanilla	1 tsp.	5 mL
Large egg	1	1
All-purpose flour	1 1/2 cups	375 mL
Baking powder	1 tsp.	5 mL
Baking soda	1/2 tsp.	2 mL
Salt	1/4 tsp.	1 mL
Buttermilk (or reconstituted from powder)	2/3 cup	150 mL
Ground cinnamon	1/2 tsp.	2 mL
Hard margarine (or butter), melted	2 tsp.	10 mL
Granulated sugar	1 tbsp.	15 mL
Ground cinnamon	1 tsp.	5 mL

Beat first 4 ingredients in medium bowl until light and creamy.

Measure next 4 ingredients into small bowl. Stir.

Add flour mixture to margarine mixture in 3 additions, alternating with buttermilk in 2 additions, beginning and ending with flour mixture. Stir until just combined. Spoon about 1/2 of batter by heaping spoonfuls randomly into greased 8 x 8 inch (20 x 20 cm) pan. Do not spread.

Sprinkle with first amount of cinnamon. Spoon remaining batter over top. Spread evenly, creating a marbled effect. Bake in 350°F (175°C) oven for about 30 minutes until wooden pick inserted in centre comes out clean. Let stand for 10 minutes.

Brush top of warm cake with melted margarine.

Combine second amounts of sugar and cinnamon in small cup. Sprinkle over cake. Serve warm. Cuts into 9 pieces.

1 piece: 268 Calories; 12.5 g Total Fat (7.8 g Mono, 1.3 g Poly, 2.7 g Sat); 25 mg Cholesterol; 35 g Carbohydrate; 1 g Fibre; 4 g Protein; 342 mg Sodium

Measurement Tables

Throughout this book measurements are given in Conventional and Metric measure. To compensate for differences between the two measurements due to rounding, a full metric measure is not always used. The cup used is the standard 8 fluid ounces. Temperature is given in degrees Fahrenheit and Celsius. Baking pan measurements are in inches and centimetres as well as quarts and litres. An exact metric conversion is given below as well as the working equivalent (Metric Standard Measure).

Spoons

Conventional Measure	Metric Exact Conversion Millilitre (mL)	Metric Standard Measure Millilitre (mL)
1/8 teaspoon (tsp.)	0.6 mL	0.5 mL
1/4 teaspoon (tsp.)	1.2 mL	1 mL
1/2 teaspoon (tsp.)	2.4 mL	2 mL
1 teaspoon (tsp.)	4.7 mL	5 mL
2 teaspoons (tsp.)	9.4 mL	10 mL
1 tablespoon (tbsp.)	14.2 mL	15 mL

Cups

Conventional Measure	Metric Exact Conversion Millilitre (mL)	Metric Standard Measure Millilitre (mL)
1/4 cup (4 tbsp.)	56.8 mL	60 mL
1/3 cup (5 1/3 tbsp.)	75.6 mL	75 mL
1/2 cup (8 tbsp.)	113.7 mL	125 mL
2/3 cup (10 2/3 tbsp.)	151.2 mL	150 mL
3/4 cup (12 tbsp.)	170.5 mL	175 mL
1 cup (16 tbsp.)	227.3 mL	250 mL
4 1/2 cups	1022.9 mL	1000 mL (1 L)

Dry Measurements

Conventional Measure Ounces (oz.)	Metric Exact Conversion Grams (g)	Metric Standard Measure Grams (g)
1 oz.	28.3 g	28 g
2 oz.	56.7 g	57 g
3 oz.	85.0 g	85 g
4 oz.	113.4 g	125 g
5 oz.	141.7 g	140 g
6 oz.	170.1 g	170 g
7 oz.	198.4 g	200 g
8 oz.	226.8 g	250 g
16 oz.	453.6 g	500 g
32 oz.	907.2 g	1000 g (1 kg)

Oven Temperatures

Fahrenheit (°F)	Celsius (°C)
175°	80°
200°	95°
225°	110°
250°	120°
275°	140°
300°	150°
325°	160°
350°	175°
375°	190°
400°	205°
425°	220°
450°	230°
475°	240°
500°	260°

Pans

Conventional Inches	Metric Centimetres
8x8 inch	20x20 cm
9x9 inch	22x22 cm
9x13 inch	22x33 cm
10x15 inch	25x38 cm
11x17 inch	28x43 cm
8x2 inch round	20x5 cm
9x2 inch round	22x5 cm
10x4 1/2 inch tube	25x11 cm
8x4x3 inch loaf	20x10x7.5 cm
9x5x3 inch loaf	22x12.5x7.5 cm

Casseroles

CANADA & BRITAIN Standard Size Casserole	Exact Metric Measure	UNITED STATES Standard Size Casserole	Exact Metric Measure
1 qt. (5 cups)	1.13 L	1 qt. (4 cups)	900 mL
1 1/2 qts. (7 1/2 cups)	1.69 L	1 1/2 qts. (6 cups)	1.35 L
2 qts. (10 cups)	2.25 L	2 qts. (8 cups)	1.8 L
2 1/2 qts. (12 1/2 cups)	2.81 L	2 1/2 qts. (10 cups)	2.25 L
3 qts. (15 cups)	3.38 L	3 qts. (12 cups)	2.7 L
4 qts. (20 cups)	4.5 L	4 qts. (16 cups)	3.6 L
5 qts. (25 cups)	5.63 L	5 qts. (20 cups)	4.5 L

Herbs Index

151

Spices Index

153

Recipe Index

155

156

Company's Coming cookbooks are available at retail locations throughout Canada!

EXCLUSIVE mail order offer on next page

Buy any 2 cookbooks—choose a 3rd FREE of equal or less value than the lowest price paid.

Original Series   CA$15.99 Canada   US$12.99 USA & International

CODE		CODE		CODE	
SQ	150 Delicious Squares	SC	Slow Cooker Recipes	RC	The Rookie Cook
CA	Casseroles	ODM	One-Dish Meals	RHR	Rush-Hour Recipes
MU	Muffins & More	ST	Starters	SW	Sweet Cravings
SA	Salads	SF	Stir-Fry	YRG	Year-Round Grilling
AP	Appetizers	MAM	Make-Ahead Meals	GG	Garden Greens
SS	Soups & Sandwiches	PB	The Potato Book	CHC	Chinese Cooking
CO	Cookies	CCLFC	Low-Fat Cooking	PK	The Pork Book
PA	Pasta	CCLFP	Low-Fat Pasta	RL	Recipes For Leftovers
BA	Barbecues	CFK	Cook For Kids	EB	The Egg Book
PR	Preserves	SCH	Stews, Chilies & Chowders	SDP	School Days Parties
CH	Chicken, Etc.	FD	Fondues	HS	Herbs & Spices
KC	Kids Cooking	CCBE	The Beef Book	BEV	The Beverage Book **NEW**
CT	Cooking For Two	CB	The Cheese Book		*October 1/04*

Lifestyle Series

CODE	CA$17.99 Canada US$15.99 USA & International
DC	Diabetic Cooking

CODE	CA$19.99 Canada US$15.99 USA & International
HC	Heart-Friendly Cooking
DDI	Diabetic Dinners

Special Occasion Series

CODE	CA$20.99 Canada US$19.99 USA & International
GFK	Gifts from the Kitchen

CODE	CA$22.99 Canada US$19.99 USA & International
WC	Weekend Cooking

CODE	CA$24.99 Canada US$19.99 USA & International
BSS	Baking—Simple to Sensational **NEW**
	September 1/04

Most Loved Recipe Collection

CODE	CA$23.99 Canada US$19.99 USA & International
MLA	Most Loved Appetizers
MLMC	Most Loved Main Courses

Company's Coming COOKBOOKS

Company's Coming Publishing Limited
2311 – 96 Street
Edmonton, Alberta, Canada T6N 1G3
Tel: 780-450-6223 Fax: 780-450-1857
www.companyscoming.com

EXCLUSIVE Mail Order Offer
See previous page for list of cookbooks

Buy**2** Get**1** FREE!
Buy any 2 cookbooks—choose a **3rd FREE**
of equal or less value than the lowest price paid.

Quantity	Code	Title	Price Each	Price Total
			$	$
		DON'T FORGET		
		to indicate your		
		FREE BOOK(S).		
		(see exclusive mail order		
		offer above)		
		please print		

TOTAL BOOKS (including FREE)

TOTAL BOOKS PURCHASED: $

	International	Canada & USA
Plus Shipping & Handling (per destination)	$11.98 (one book)	$5.98 (one book)
Additional Books (including FREE books)	$ ($4.99 each)	$ ($1.99 each)
Sub-Total	$	$
Canadian residents add G.S.T.(7%)		$
TOTAL AMOUNT ENCLOSED	$	$

The Fine Print
- Orders outside Canada must be **PAID IN US FUNDS** by cheque or money order drawn on Canadian or US bank or by credit card.
- Make cheque or money order payable to: **Company's Coming Publishing Limited.**
- Prices are expressed in Canadian dollars for Canada, US dollars for USA & International and are subject to change without prior notice.
- Orders are shipped surface mail. For courier rates, visit our web-site: **www.companyscoming.com** or contact us: **Tel: 780-450-6223 Fax: 780-450-1857.**
- Sorry, no C.O.D.'s.

Gift Giving
- Let us help you with your gift giving!
- We will send cookbooks directly to the recipients of your choice if you give us their names and addresses.
- Please specify the titles you wish to send to each person.
- If you would like to include your personal note or card, we will be pleased to enclose it with your gift order.
- Company's Coming Cookbooks make excellent gifts: Birthdays, bridal showers, Mother's Day, Father's Day, graduation or any occasion ...collect them all!

☐ MasterCard ☐ VISA

_____
Expiry date

Account # _____

Name of cardholder _____

Cardholder's signature _____

Shipping Address
Send the cookbooks listed above to:

Name: _____

Street: _____

City: _____ Prov./State: _____

Country: _____ Postal Code/Zip: _____

Tel: (_____) _____

Email address: _____

☐ YES! Please send a catalogue

Boost your breakfast with something cold and fruity or pour something warm and relaxing after supper. *The Beverage Book* is perfect for everyday fare or entertaining family and friends.

In this book:
- Breakfast Drinks
- Coffee & Tea Drinks
- Frozen & Juicer Drinks
- Holiday & Theme Drinks
- Punches & Pitcher Drinks
- Kids' Drinks & more!

Quick
&
Easy
Recipes

Everyday
Ingredients

Canada's
most popular
cookbooks!